Søren Kierkegaard's
Christian Psychology

Also by C. Stephen Evans . . .
*The Quest for Faith: Reason & Mystery as
Pointers to God*
*Preserving the Person: A Look at
the Human Sciences*
*Existentialism: The Philosophy of Despair and the
Quest for Hope*

Søren Kierkegaard's Christian Psychology

Insight for Counseling and Pastoral Care

C. Stephen Evans

REGENT COLLEGE PUBLISHING
VANCOUVER, BRITISH COLUMBIA

SØREN KIERKEGAARD'S CHRISTIAN PSYCHOLOGY
Copyright © 1990 by C. Stephan Evans

Original edition published 1990
under the imprint MINISTRY RESOURCES LIBRARY
of Zondervan Publishing House, 1415 Lake Drive S.E.,
Grand Rapids MI 49506   (ISBN 0-310-43751-2)

All Scripture, unless otherwise noted, are directly quoted from the HOLY BIBLE:
NEW INTERNATIONAL VERSION (North American Edition). Copyright
1973, 1978, 1984, by the International Bible Society.
Used by permission of Zondervan Bible Publishers.

This edition published with permission
by Regent College Publishing, an imprint of the Regent College Bookstore,
5800 University Boulevard, Vancouver, B.C. V6T 2E4 Canada

Printed in Canada

Both feminine and masculine pronouns are used generically in this book.

First printing   1995
Second printing 1997

Library of Congress Cataloguing in Publication Data

Evans, C. Stephen.
    Søren Kierkegaard's Christian Psychology / C. Stephen Evans.
        p.   cm.
    Includes bibliographical references.
    1. Christianity–Psychology–History of doctrines–20th century.
2. Kierkegaard, Søren, 1813-1855–Contributions in Christian psychology.
3. Psychology–Methodology–Religious aspects–Christianity–History of
doctrines–19th century. I. Title.
BR110.E915   1995
201'.9–DC20

ISBN 1-57383-038-0

To Stanton Jones
who takes seriously the ideal
of Christian psychology

CONTENTS

PREFACE

Søren Kierkegaard was and is an enigma. Misunderstood and largely ignored during his lifetime, he was discovered and celebrated in the twentieth century, though mainly for reasons he would have deplored. Today Kierkegaard is a difficult figure to ignore. He continues to tempt and allure. The range of his writings, covering philosophy, theology, psychology, sociology, and literary criticism, as well as lyrical poetic productions and edifying religious works, produces the unmistakable impression that one has encountered true genius. The size and variety of that production, partially masked in pseudonyms and heavily laced with humor and irony, overwhelms the reader.

It is not surprising, then, that there seem to be as many ways of reading Kierkegaard as there are readers of Kierkegaard. In the fifties Kierkegaard was seen as the father of existentialism, the forerunner of Sartre, Camus, and Heidegger. Today he is read as the first "post-modern" writer, a predecessor to Derrida, who shows us the death of the author and all "author-ity."

The richness and poetic openness of Kierkegaard's writings make possible such readings and in one sense legitimizes them. Kierkegaard would agree with Derrida that an author is not necessarily the best interpreter of his own work and that authorship has a certain public status. Once completed, a work stands by itself and in a sense is whatever people make of it. So perhaps Kierkegaard would not mind what people have made of his writings, so long as those people are willing to accept responsibility for their creative shaping.

However, I believe that there is great value in reading Kierkegaard "straight," looking at his works in the way he himself preferred to look at them, rather than seeing him as a precursor of some intellectual movement or as an influence on various philosophical traditions. This is so, not because Kierkegaard himself has any authority—an idea he would have been the first to disown—but simply because this way of looking at his writings has much to say to us as individuals and as a society. The argument is not that we must read Kierkegaard in a certain way because that is the way he wanted to be read, but that we should read Kierkegaard in a certain way because when we do, we discover things about ourselves and our world we would otherwise miss.

But how did Kierkegaard want to be read? There is little question that Kierkegaard saw himself first and foremost as a Christian author. He tried to write as an individual for individuals, to challenge people to think hard about the innermost regions of their lives. He did not believe that Christian faith could grow in superficial soil. In this book I try to take both Kierkegaard's Christian faith and his personal challenge seriously.

This is a book about Kierkegaard as a psychologist. That might seem like an academic topic, but the book is not primarily for scholars. In fact, Kierkegaard specialists will probably find little that is new here. Instead I have tried to write it for psychologists, pastors, counselors, and ordinary people struggling to understand themselves and others.

It is appropriate to approach Kierkegaard's psychology in this manner because for Kierkegaard, psychology was not a narrow or heavy academic enterprise. For him its study could not be separated from the task of personal becoming. His own struggle to become a Christian involved a struggle to understand himself and what it means to be and become a person. I shall try to look at the psychological lessons he learned, but I cannot and would not wish to detach those lessons from his personal struggle or his challenge to us.

The organization of the present book is, for the most part, straightforward. I should like to mention, however, that chapter 2, which deals with some methodological issues and may be more difficult than the other chapters, could be omitted by readers mainly interested in the content of Kierkegaard's thought. Yet readers who are interested in the question of whether there could be a distinctively Christian approach to psychology as a discipline may find that chapter especially interesting.

In conclusion I would like to express my deep thanks to Stanton Jones and Robert Roberts of Wheaton College. Each gave generously of his time to read and criticize an early version of this book.

—C. Stephen Evans
St. Olaf College

ACKNOWLEDGMENTS

The author is grateful to the publishers for permission to use the following:

Portions of chapter 2 are adapted from the book *Wisdom and Humanness in Psychology* by C. Stephen Evans, copyright © 1989, published by Baker Book House, Grand Rapids, Michigan.

Extensive quotations from *The Sickness unto Death: A Christian Psychological Exposition for Upbuilding and Awakening*, by Søren Kierkegaard, copyright © 1980 by Princeton University Press, edited and translated by Howard V. Hong and Edna H. Hong, are used with permission of Princeton University Press, Princeton, New Jersey.

CHAPTER 1

Kierkegaard as a Christian

Psychologists have often been more interested in Kierkegaard as a subject for analysis than as a theorist, and he has been variously diagnosed as paranoid, schizoid, and manic-depressive, to mention just a few labels.[1] In this book we are interested in Kierkegaard's psychological insights, but like the analysts, we must begin with his life. After all, one of his lessons for us is that we theorize as whole persons, not detached egos, so it is important to view his activity as a psychologist against the background of his own struggles.

Kierkegaard's Life

Throughout his life Kierkegaard suffered a great deal from what he called his "melancholy." Today we would call it depression.

Even as a child, Kierkegaard was unusually reflective and introspective, prone to feelings of deep sadness covered over by a witty outer personality: "So far back as I can barely remember, my one joy was that nobody could discover how unhappy I felt."[2] He describes his own childhood as "crazy, humanly speaking,"[3] and laments his failure to experience what he (somewhat idealistically perhaps) describes as the innocent "immediacy" of childhood.[4]

Born in 1813 in Copenhagen, Kierkegaard was brought up

in a strict, pietistic Lutheran home by a somewhat elderly father. The father was a well-to-do, retired merchant, who was himself riddled by guilt and depression. The father's first wife died after a brief marriage. Very soon after this, he married one of the servants, with the first child of this marriage arriving about four months after the wedding.

Sometime in his early twenties Søren Kierkegaard speaks in his *Journal* of "the great earthquake" when he had discovered his father's guilty secret or secrets.[5] What these secrets were, no one knows for sure, but a good guess is that they concerned the father's sexual indiscretions. An additional possibility revolves around an incident from his father's childhood. When the father was a penniless shepherd on the west side of Jutland, bitter about his loneliness and sufferings, the boy had climbed a hill and cursed God. From this time on, the father's fortunes mysteriously improved. Nevertheless, the father never forgot his youthful act of defiance and in later life was apparently gripped by the conviction that he had committed the unpardonable sin.

These guilty feelings in the father were increased when five of his seven children died within a relatively short time. The father became convinced that God was punishing the whole family and that he was destined to outlive all his children. Much of this had doubtless been guessed or dimly intuited by his youngest child, Søren, earlier, but the "great earthquake" confirmed and sharpened the gifted, reflective young man's bent to melancholy.

What made the situation doubly tragic was that Søren felt he had in some way already repeated his father's sins, that in some sense his father's guilt had been truly visited upon him. In his student years at the university, Søren had reacted strongly against his strict Christian upbringing, and it is doubtless during this period that he had "sowed his wild oats." Just prior to his father's death, around his twenty-fifth birthday, Kierkegaard was reconciled with his father and came back to his faith. However, for the rest of his life Kierkegaard considered himself a penitent. Though he acquired more confidence of God's forgiveness of sins in Christ as he grew older, his painful awareness of his own deficiencies led him to view himself as a "very mediocre Christian."[6] Often, in fact, to emphasize the extent to which the Christian life is a process, he speaks of himself as one who is in process of *becoming* a Christian.

There were two great events in Kierkegaard's life that decisively shaped his work as an author. The first was his broken engagement, an event which precipitated his most significant early works and which, in his own words, "made him a poet." Kierkegaard had met Regine Olsen when she was just fourteen and he was twenty-four. He fell desperately in love, and a few years later—after he had completed his advanced degree in theology, which would have prepared him for a career in the church—he wooed her and won from her a promise of marriage.

The whole affair was a dreadful mistake. Kierkegaard loved Regine deeply and continued to do so until his death. He hoped that through marriage to her he could break out of his introversion and melancholic reflectiveness. However, he saw very soon that he had erred; he could not be a husband. He believed strongly that marriage was an equal partnership in which mutual understanding and self-disclosure were essential. Yet he could not reveal himself to Regine. To explain his own psychological torments he would have to disclose his family history, and this he felt would be a violation of his now-deceased father.

After an anguished period he finally made a clean break. He tried (unsuccessfully, in Regine's eyes at least) to portray himself as a cad in order to wean her away from him and make the break easier for her. Still hoping and praying for a miracle, some change in himself that would make marriage possible, he fled to Berlin for a period, thinking that his case might be similar to that of Abraham and Isaac, in which Abraham's willingness to offer up Isaac was rewarded with the return of Isaac. But alas, Kierkegaard's "Isaac" was not to return. When he returned to Copenhagen he found Regine engaged to another man!

Whether or not we approve of Kierkegaard's conduct in this affair, it is certain that these experiences decisively shaped his authorship. He began to write books "for her," dedicated to "that individual," who is described as "one unnamed who will someday be named."

The books were of two kinds. There was a series of books, ascribed to pseudonyms, which Kierkegaard described as "aesthetic" in character. In *Either-Or, Fear and Trembling,* and *Repetition,* Kierkegaard explores the nature of human passion in a variety of forms, often presenting his own experiences in a poetically disguised narrative. He hoped to reveal himself at last to Regine in this "indirect" manner. Several other pseudonymous books followed, some of which are more overtly philosophical in character.

At the same time that these aesthetic writings were being published, Kierkegaard wrote a series of edifying, sermonlike essays, though he was careful to insist that they were not sermons, in part because he had not been ordained and therefore lacked "authority." Through these he communicated his underlying religious commitments in a more "direct" fashion. Kierkegaard continued to write these "edifying discourses" throughout his life, but as he grew older they focused on more distinctively Christian themes and took on a decidedly sharper tone. Both for the pseudonymous, aesthetic authorship and the edifying, religious writings, what began at least partially as an attempt to communicate "to her" very soon (if not from the beginning) took on a broader, more universal meaning. "The individual" became not just a particular person, but a distinctive philosophical category.

The second external event that was decisive for Kierkegaard's life and writings was an encounter with a satirical periodical, *The Corsair.* The periodical, which is perhaps best described as somewhere between *Mad Magazine* and *Punch,* had won a huge following by pillorying the leading citizens of Denmark. In 1846 Kierkegaard had just completed his *Concluding Unscientific Postscript,* which, as the title implies, he had intended to be his final production. His thought was that he would then take a country parish and finish his days in peace and relative solitude.

The Corsair had until this time spared Kierkegaard its barbs, since the editor had a genuine admiration for him. Kierkegaard himself thought the paper was irresponsible, and he was especially upset over the way one of the writers, whom he knew, hid his involvement with the periodical. In a short piece, Kierkegaard exposed this person's involvement and begged to be spared the embarrassment of being the only notable person in Denmark who was *not* ridiculed in *The Corsair.*

The paper took up this challenge with zest, making Søren the butt of almost every issue for the next year. His physical appearance was particularly savaged, and such items as the length of his trousers were made the focus of many a cartoon. Kierkegaard, who had until then found his chief recreation in walking about the streets of Copenhagen and who had made a special point of being respectful and friendly to the common person, soon found it impossible to go anywhere, even to church, without crowds of gawking, jeering onlookers. Anyone would have found this trying, but to a person of Kierkegaard's temperament, it was all but unbearable.

Out of the suffering of this period emerged a new religious sensitivity. Kierkegaard now came to believe that it would be cowardly to retire to a country parish. He must "remain at his post." His edifying religious writings from this period show a new appreciation of the place of suffering in the Christian life. He had always been acquainted with suffering and had always understood its importance in the religious life, but now he was forced to confront a new kind of suffering— *voluntary* suffering, incurred when a Christian takes a stand against the world and is willing to endure persecution for it.

Almost from the beginning of his authorship Kierkegaard had waged a battle against what he termed "Christendom." Christendom, epitomized in the state church of Denmark, represented establishment Christianity. In Christendom we are all Christians, but our Christianity comes cheaply and means nothing. If you are born in a Christian country and you aren't Jewish, then you must be a Christian. To be a distinguished Christian is simply to be a distinguished citizen, to live a decent, tasteful life, but one that is in no way distinctive. For Kierkegaard, the error of Christendom was the most dangerous error of all with respect to true Christianity. As long as people are lulled into thinking they are already Christians by being born into Christendom, they are prevented from becoming true Christians.

After the controversy with *The Corsair,* Kierkegaard's attack on Christendom took on a new urgency. He came to see more clearly the power of the media and the difficulty of existing as an authentic individual in modern society. A true Christian is not just an admirer of Jesus, but a *follower*, and this requires a willingness to stand up against any earthly power and to sacrifice any earthly good. Finally, in 1854 Kierkegaard began a public attack on the state church and the ideal of "Christendom" it represented. Lamenting that New Testament Christianity had ceased to exist, he demanded that people at least be honest with God. In no way did he think that people could earn or merit salvation through their own efforts; it is all God's doing. But the least we owe to God is an honest admission before we take refuge in grace.

In the midst of the fire-storm he began, Kierkegaard collapsed on the street. He had just withdrawn the last of the fortune he had inherited and had finished the last issue of a periodical he had started as a vehicle for his attack. Just forty-two years old, he was taken to a hospital and died a few weeks later, on November 11, 1855. He refused to take Communion from a representative of the state church, but resolutely affirmed to a priest who was a boyhood friend that his hope and trust was solely in God's grace in Christ.

Kierkegaard's Mission

Kierkegaard saw himself as a religious author. In *The Point of View for My Work as an Author*, he argues against the superficial reading of his work as an "aesthetic" author (an author whose basic concerns are literary in nature) who eventually became religious.[7] It is true that many of Kierkegaard's early writings, beginning with *Either-Or*, are pseudonymous and have a rich aesthetic flavor, and it is true that Kierkegaard's later writings tend to have a more pronounced religious, and specifically Christian, content and tone. However, Kierkegaard asserts that the best explanation for this is not that he began as an aesthetic author and changed to a religious one. Certainly his religious faith changed and deepened over the years, but he was from the beginning a religious author. The early aesthetic writings are themselves religiously inspired,[8] part of a strategy Kierkegaard had adopted.

This strategy was tailored to Kierkegaard's mission,

which was, he claimed, "the reintroduction of Christianity into Christendom."[9] He considered "Christendom"—the assumption that "we are all Christians"—a monstrous illusion that blocked people from an understanding of true Christianity and therefore effectively prevented them from becoming true Christians. As Kierkegaard saw it, the majority of people in Christendom, while imagining themselves to be Christians, actually live in what he called aesthetic categories.[10] That is, their deepest concerns in life are pleasure and pain, fortune and misfortune. People like this cannot be expected to be directly interested in the kinds of spiritual issues Christianity regards as crucial, so Kierkegaard begins with a kind of pious deception.[11]

In a variety of ways Kierkegaard attempted to engage his readers aesthetically, though the works have an underlying moral and religious purpose. The "deception," as he called it, could be viewed simply as sugarcoating the medicine, but it really is more than this. If Christianity is the medicine, Kierkegaard saw it as his job to help his reader develop the capacities that would enable the medicine to work. Through his aesthetic authorship, he attempted to develop those qualities—which he termed "seriousness" and "inwardness"—in his readers, qualities that are the essential preconditions for understanding Christianity and becoming a Christian. Thus he claimed that the whole of his authorship, not just the obviously religious section, was "related to Christianity, to the problem of becoming a Christian, with a direct or indirect polemic against the monstrous illusion we call Christendom."[12]

Therefore Kierkegaard is best understood, not primarily as a philosopher, psychologist, theologian, literary critic, or poet, but as a missionary to the pagans in Christendom, those who took it for granted that they were Christians. Of course, he was also a psychologist, but we must understand that role in light of his primary mission.

The Need for Psychology

Kierkegaard regarded psychology as decisively important. To understand why, we must try to understand his view of Christian faith. As Kierkegaard saw it, Christianity is not primarily a matter of intellectually knowing or believing certain doctrines, nor is it primarily having certain momentary feelings or experiences. It is a way of living, or, as Kierkegaard himself preferred to put it, a way of *existing*. It is certainly true that Christians believe some things which non-Christians do not, so the doctrines of the faith are not unimportant. But the crucial thing to see is that Christians do not merely believe with their heads; they believe with their hearts. This means that the doctrines of Christianity are only truly believed when they are capable of moving the person to action, for it is in our actions that the whole person is revealed. To believe that Jesus is Lord in the Christian way is not merely to assent to a proposition; it is to have your life transformed in a radical manner.

Why should anyone want to become a Christian? The reasons will not be primarily intellectual. The most basic decisions we humans make about the direction of our lives are always rooted in what we care most deeply about. To become a Christian a person must care about eternal life.

But who does not care about eternal life? Wouldn't everyone like to live forever? Perhaps, at a superficial level. But Christianity conceives of eternal life not simply as something to be acquired beyond the grave; it is also a new quality of life to be acquired in the here and now. And few seem to want it most in this life.

What most people want most are temporal goods: houses, automobiles, membership in the club, prestigious jobs, power, and sex. People who want these things most of all have difficulty getting too excited about eternal life. When they try to conceive of eternal life, they naturally think of it as an endless extension of the kind of life they enjoy now. But such an endless extension can seem very distant and unreal and, to tell the truth, even boring. Many temporal activities take on a different character if we truly think of ourselves as carrying them on for eternity.

According to Kierkegaard, what is really attractive about eternal life, Christianly conceived, is that it will provide an endless opportunity to enjoy God as God has made himself known in Christ. This is only really attractive to those who love God, those who would genuinely enjoy his company. These are the same people, of course, who abhor sin and who see the separation from God that is the result of sin as hell.

Now one might think that the task of the evangelist or "missionary to Christendom" would be to make people desire to know God so they would be more likely to turn to Christ, and that a knowledge of psychology would be helpful for this. This would be a mistake, however, since only God can truly induce a desire for himself. Still, we are in the neighborhood of the truth at this point.

Only God can instill a desire for himself in a human being. Yet there is a sense in which God has already done this for everyone. He has placed a desire for eternity in the human heart. He has created us in such a way that we cannot find our ultimate happiness apart from himself. This deep truth makes it impossible to separate Kierkegaard the missionary, interested in helping people find God, from Kierkegaard the psychologist, interested in helping people become healthy and happy. It is true that most of us do not realize God has planted this deep desire within us, or at least we do not realize it clearly. It is also true that we have conflicting desires; God is the one whom we do not wish to know, and so our need for him is one we do not easily acknowledge.

Nevertheless, there are symptoms of our deepest need present in our lives. Here is where the psychologist can be helpful to the "spiritual physician." The psychologist can help us see these symptoms for what they truly are and thereby can help us move toward greater self-understanding.

This greater self-understanding does not necessarily or automatically lead to Christian faith. A person may see his need for God and self-consciously rebel against God. Self-understanding can lead to defiance as well as humble faith. But self-understanding at least makes faith a live possibility. If we understand that we are spiritual beings, intended for eternal life, then we have the option of seeking our true destinies or decisively rejecting our true selves.

Kierkegaard likes to put the matter like this: Christianity is the solution to *the* problem of human existence. Most of his contemporaries did not understand Christianity because they did not understand human existence profoundly enough. One cannot understand the solution without understanding the problem.

So although Kierkegaard's mission was to reintroduce Christianity into Christendom, he saw psychology as an essential element in that task. Before he could begin to communicate Christianity to people, he had to help them gain a truer perspective on what it means to exist as a human being.

I do not mean to imply that Kierkegaard was interested in psychology solely as a kind of pre-evangelistic aid. In fact, even to describe the matter in such a way presupposes a view of the psychological and the spiritual as unrelated, a view that Kierkegaard firmly rejected. Like contemporary psychologists, Kierkegaard was interested in why people behave as they do, how they achieve fulfillment, and how they go wrong in their lives. And he was interested in these issues for their own sakes. However, he also recognized their significance for the evangelist and the missionary, not to mention the Christian education worker and Christian parent. And of course he also recognized the value of the gospel proclaimed by the evangelist and missionary for the work of the psychologist.

The major thrust of Kierkegaard's early pseudonymous writings is, broadly speaking, psychological in that they focus on helping people gain a sense of what it means to exist as whole persons. The reason for the pseudonymity of these writings is linked to this goal. The pseudonymous "authors" of Kierkegaard's early works are not just pen names for him to hide behind. They are *personae*, like characters in a novel. Like literary characters they have their own perspectives and views, which are not necessarily identical with Kierkegaard's personal beliefs. Kierkegaard created these characters to represent what he saw as fundamental human possibilities. In holding out these characters to his readers he was therefore not simply presenting opinions, but possible mirrors. He hoped that his readers would look into these works, behold themselves, and discover something about their own spiritual character.

In these works Kierkegaard explored the depths of the human heart, particularly its emotions and passions. As we shall see, he saw the best clues to our eternal destiny in the emotions of anxiety and despair. The key to becoming a

Christian lay in the development of the right kinds of passions, especially the all-important Christian passions of faith, hope, and love.

At this point we may reasonably ask what Kierkegaard meant by "psychology." Does this psychology, which is to be the handmaiden of evangelism in Christendom, have anything to do with what is called psychology today? What, if anything, can Christian psychologists today learn from Kierkegaard? These are questions we shall confront in the next chapter.

Notes

1. For examples see Ib Ostenfeld, *Søren Kierkegaard's Psychology* (Waterloo, Ontario: Wilfrid Laurier University Press, 1978); Hjalmar Helweg, *Søren Kierkegaard, En psykiatrisk-psykologisk studie* (Copenhagen: Hagerup, 1933); John Bjorkhem, *Søren Kierkegaard in psykologisk belysning* (Uppsala: Nyblom, 1942); and Josiah Thompson, *Kierkegaard* (New York: Alfred Knopf, 1973).

2. Søren Kierkegaard, *The Point of View for My Work as an Author,* trans. Walter Lowrie (New York: Harper & Row, 1962), 76 (hereafter *The Point of View*).

3. Ibid., 76.

4. Ibid., 81.

5. *Søren Kierkegaard's Journals and Papers,* vol. 5, ed. and trans. Howard V. Hong and Edna H. Hong (Bloomington: Indiana University Press, 1978), entry 5430.

6. Ibid., entry 6431.

7. Kierkegaard, *The Point of View,* 10–11.

8. Ibid., 5–6.

9. Ibid., 23.

10. Ibid., 25.

11. Ibid., 39–41.

12. Ibid., 5–6.

CHAPTER 2

Kierkegaard as a Psychologist

Kierkegaard regarded himself as a psychologist. Three of his books, *The Concept of Anxiety*, *Repetition*, and *The Sickness unto Death*, are designated as psychological by their subtitles, and he frequently called himself a psychologist in his journal.

Yet it is evident that Kierkegaard was quite different in many ways from most contemporary psychologists. To mention just one point, albeit a significant one, we have seen that Kierkegaard viewed psychology as an essential tool for evangelism, or what might be termed pre-evangelism. This is a perspective that seems far removed from the value-neutral stance of contemporary academic psychology. Even clinical psychologists may well wonder about the relevance of Kierkegaard in this connection. If Kierkegaard is primarily an evangelist, they may think, then he and I are essentially in different lines of work, even if we labor for the same firm. So how can Kierkegaard fruitfully serve as a model for Christian psychologists in our time?

It is obvious that Kierkegaard cannot serve as a model for psychology as it is currently practiced; he could only be a model for what psychology could become. To ask what psychology could become, however, we must first think critically about the prevailing conception of psychology today.

Let us begin by attempting to take a naive attitude toward the issue. Imagine a naive Christian who knows nothing about psychology as a science—let's call him "Kirk"—engaged in conversation with a knowledgeable psychologist—"Dr. John."

Dr. John tells Kirk that psychology models itself after the natural sciences and attempts to gain a scientific understanding of human behavior and mental processes.

Kirk asks Dr. John what psychologists think about God and God's relationship to human beings. Dr. John replies that individual psychologists have different beliefs about God. He himself is a Christian, he tells Kirk, and of course, for him any ultimate understanding of human begins requires a theological perspective too. But, he hastens to add, his personal religious beliefs do not enter into psychology as a scientific discipline because science restricts itself to the natural realm, which can be studied by empirical methods.

Dr. John's answer leaves Kirk dissatisfied. He has a lot of lingering misgivings. Kirk can understand that science may have to limit itself to the empirically observable, but he questions the value, or even the truthfulness, of the knowledge gained by such a science. After all, he thinks, isn't the most important thing about human beings their relationship to God? Can anyone hope to understand them without understanding them in this light?

Kirk is willing to entertain the possibility of studying aspects of God's creation apart from an explicit understanding of God. Perhaps, he thinks, that's possible in the physical sciences like physics, chemistry, and biology, but humans aren't purely physical creatures. Surely the nonbiological aspects of human beings are heavily shaped by their relationships with others—including God. He suspects that any science that focuses on human beings and ignores the Creator would be in trouble.

I do not mean to suggest that Dr. John is wrong here and Kirk is right. But I do think that the questions Kirk asks are very good ones and that we would all profit from asking those questions again with a certain naïveté.

I believe that most Christian psychologists are implicitly aware of some tension between their theological understanding of human persons and their perspectives as psychologists.

The usual strategy for dealing with the issue is the adoption of what I have termed the "limiter of science" approach.[1] Of course science takes a limited perspective; it must to remain science. However, no harm is done so long as we recognize the limitations of science and also recognize the need for other perspectives to get a full picture of human beings. The scientific perspective is valid and useful, but the perspectives of the theologian, the novelist, the artist, and the philosopher have validity as well.

The limiter of science must be contrasted with the humanizer of science, who takes a different tack. The humanizer rejects the assumption of the limiter that the human sciences must pattern themselves on the older natural sciences; he asserts that psychology, as a human science, must employ unique methods to do justice to its unique subject.

There is a good deal of the limiter of science in Kierkegaard. A prominent theme in his writings is that science is valid in its place, but cannot deal with the most basic and ultimate questions of life. Science is necessarily objective, and objectivity has a legitimate place in life, but there is another kind of knowledge or insight that is essentially subjective in character and cannot be gained through scientific study. This is the side of Kierkegaard most discussed in books about him.

There is another strand to Kierkegaard's thought, however, and this strand is emphatically that of the humanizer. It comes through most prominently in *The Sickness unto Death*.

In the preface to *The Sickness unto Death* the pseudonymous author Anti-Climacus says that "many will perhaps find the form of this 'exposition' strange; it will seem to them too rigorous to be edifying and too edifying to be scientific in the strict sense" (p. 5).[2] Anti-Climacus says he has no opinion about the latter charge, but he defends himself against the former. It is true, of course, that not everyone will be able to understand the work, so it will not be edifying to everyone, but this does not mean the work itself is not properly edifying (p. 5).

We might think that the relative indifference of Anti-Climacus to the charge that his work is too edifying to be scientific would be evidence that he holds to a limiter-of-science perspective. However, he goes on to undermine this hasty first impression with a withering attack on the whole enterprise of disinterested science:

From a Christian point of view, everything, absolutely everything, must serve for edification. That type of scientific knowledge which is in the end unedifying, is precisely thereby unchristian. . . . This Christian relationship to life (in contrast to a scientific remoteness from life), or this ethical side of Christianity is precisely the edifying, and this type of production, however rigorous it may otherwise be, is absolutely different, qualitatively different from that type of scientific knowledge, which is "indifferent," whose exalted status is, seen Christianly, so far from being heroism, that it is Christianly a type of inhuman curiosity. . . . All Christian knowledge, however rigorous it may be in form, ought to be concerned, but this concern is precisely the edifying (p. 5).

Here we see that Kierkegaard,[3] or his pseudonym Anti-Climacus, is far from being a limiter of science who accepts objective science as being in order as long as it recognizes its limits. To someone who objects to his procedure on the grounds that it is too edifying to be scientific he offers no reply. But in the context of the remarks which follow it becomes clear that the reason he offers no reply is that he has nothing to say to such a person, who evidently has a view of science which is completely alien to Kierkegaard's own. The objector obviously holds, with Hegel, that science must beware of the wish to be edifying. In more contemporary terms, science must be value-neutral or even value-free. Kierkegaard rejects this kind of science as "inhuman curiosity" and proposes to offer instead a kind of "Christian knowing" whose hallmark is concern, in this context clearly a concern for human beings.

The Myth of the Scientific Method

Our initial question as to whether Kierkegaard can be a model for contemporary psychology is still with us, because the idea of a psychology whose primary characteristic is concern still goes against the self-image of psychology as a science, dominant in academic psychology and, though much weaker in applied psychology, still influential enough to make an explicitly religious psychology seem "unscientific" and therefore not really psychology. Psychology as a science is supposed to discover the objective truth about human nature, truth based on empirical fact. Perhaps *psychologists* should be concerned about their fellow humans, but not *psychology* as such.

The chief problem here is the continued acceptance by many psychologists of what I term the myth of *the* scientific method. I hasten to say that in attacking this myth I am neither attacking science nor denying that there are recognizable scientific methods. The myth of the scientific method is the belief that there is a single method of verification that makes one's acceptance of a theory rational. In this view what makes a theory scientific is that it can be verified or, in the greater number of cases, falsified by empirical data. There may be other, nonscientific avenues to truth, such as revelation or intuition, but these avenues cannot be employed by psychology as such, since psychology owes its existence to a commitment to the scientific method.

The picture of science that is embodied in this myth is now thoroughly discredited,[4] yet the myth survives robustly—which is strong evidence that it is indeed functioning as a myth. It is true that most psychologists now give lip service to the claim that data are themselves theory-laden and that in any case theories are always underdetermined by data. Nevertheless the typical introduction to a psychology textbook piously repeats the claim that psychology arose as a science when psychologists ceased to speculate about human behavior and began to make careful observations of facts. Our prescientific ancestors are seen as possessing occasional, lucky insights mixed with profound ignorance and downright foolishness.

Psychologists such as Mary Stewart Van Leeuwen who have questioned the myth have been received with suspicion and hostility. In at least one case Van Leeuwen has been grouped with "anti-psychologists" like Jay Adams for her temerity in suggesting that there are alternative methodologies for psychologists to follow.[5]

If the myth of the scientific method is credible, then Kierkegaard cannot be a role model for Christian psychologists today, for it is obvious that Kierkegaard did not do psychological research along empiricist lines. He did not design laboratory experiments or gather data to be analyzed quantitatively. Even his "clinical" observations often lack "objectivity," since they often presuppose Christian insights. So to make my case I must challenge this myth.

I do not want to do so in the standard way, however, by directly attacking the empiricist view of science. I believe that the case against a standard empiricist view of science is as strong as anyone could reasonably expect, and this case has been thoroughly laid out in other writings.[6] Rather, I want to attempt to relieve some of the anxiety that makes the myth so powerful.

My own hunch is that the power of the myth is linked to the socialization experiences that psychologists undergo in graduate school. There they absorb the myth as they form their identity as psychologists and are taught to think of their profession and of themselves as members of the profession in the language of the myth. Any attack on the myth is experienced as an attack on their personal identity. People who urge that psychology adopt a new paradigm or at least allow for a plurality of paradigms are perceived as calling for those in the profession now to repudiate their own work and their own identity.

While I am sympathetic to those who believe that something like a paradigm shift in psychology is desirable, I believe that a change in tactics is necessary if this goal is to be accomplished. I shall presently be arguing that psychology must put a great deal more emphasis on what I will term interpretive and critical elements in the discipline. In doing so, I will not call for a new interpretive, critical approach to supplant or even supplement the standard empiricist approach. Rather, I will argue that the empiricist approach already includes interpretive, critical elements. These elements are ineradicable from the study of human beings. The problem with the empiricist approach is not that it excludes interpretive, critical elements, but that it does not include them in a self-conscious, explicit way.

The advantage of this approach is that it does not require the empiricist to repudiate his identity or regard his previous work as without value. Instead, it offers a new perspective on that work, a perspective that brings to the forefront elements which were there all the time, but tended to be ignored or minimized.

The Three Faces of Psychology

We can think of psychology as having three faces or dimensions: the empirical dimension, the interpretive dimension, and the value-critical dimension.[7] Though these are often described as three rival approaches or views of what the discipline should be, I prefer to think of them as mutually helpful strands in a single enterprise. The disagreements between the proponents of rival approaches at best represent disagreements of emphasis, because each of the three dimensions presupposes the others. An approach that used only one of the three would be strictly impossible.

The heart of the empiricist side of psychology is the search for regularities. Examples of this kind of work can be multiplied without much effort. Are certain practices of child disciplining associated with particular forms of socially deviant behavior? Can successful performance in school be successfully predicted from performance on a certain type of standardized test? Is racial prejudice correlated with religious commitment?

The interpretive face of psychology can be seen most clearly when a psychologist seeks to understand the meaning of an action. Is a suicide attempt an act of political protest, a cry for help, an act of aggression, an expression of despair, or all of the above? Understanding the meaning of human behavior requires understanding the normative rules that human beings consciously or unconsciously follow or fail to follow, and the concepts embedded in those rules that human beings employ to understand their own actions. One might think that understanding such rules and concepts could be accomplished simply through empirical research, but this is not so. A rule is not simply a regularity, and understanding a concept is something that empirical research presupposes and does not establish.

The value-critical side of psychology, while certainly present, is probably the least developed of the three aspects in contemporary North American psychology. This aspect comes to the fore when psychologists go beyond discovering regularities and understanding rules and begin to ask who makes the rules and who sets up the reinforcers and punishers that regulate the regularities. Whose interests are being served, and are those interests being served at the expense of others' interests and the well-being of society as a whole or even the human community as a whole? For example, are the rules, implicit and explicit, that govern the role of "wife and mother" exploitative of women? Do the rules that govern the role of "liberated woman" function so as to undermine the family?

I believe that each of these three sides to the human sciences is not only legitimate, but is also dependent on the others. If, for example, a humanistic or Marxist psychologist were to claim that empirical research of the standard type was useless or harmful, I would argue that such a view is profoundly mistaken.

For my present purposes, however, I do not need to argue for the legitimacy of empirical research. Kierkegaard is unlikely to be attacked for being too empiricist. The objection to seeing Kierkegaard as a role model for psychology is likely to come from the empiricist who doubts the value of the interpretive and critical work that Kierkegaard has done.

What I must argue, therefore, is that the empiricist cannot do without the interpretive and critical dimensions. If that is correct, and if Kierkegaard has helpful things to teach us in those two areas, then his lack of empirical research will not be a fatal barrier to learning things from him that will be relevant to contemporary psychology.

So how can the case be made that standard empiricist psychology, with its rigorous methodology and statistical sophistication, has an interpretive or hermeneutical dimension which is every bit as ineradicable as the musings of a Carl Rogers or a Viktor Frankl? The hermeneutical dimension may not be as prominent or decisively important in a straightforward empirical study as it is in existential psychology (or again it may be equally important), yet it is there nevertheless.[8] Space precludes detailed illustrations, but let me list some of the places to look.

The interpretive dimension in an ordinary empirical study is present in the *operational definitions* given key concepts, in the decisions about which correlations represent *causal relations*, in decisions about the *direction of causation*, and in decisions about the larger *meaning, generalizability,* significance, and relevance of the empirical findings. Careful analysis of virtually any well-known psychological experiment, such as the famous (and ethically infamous) Milgram experiment on obedience and authority,[9] would show this clearly. No analysis of this experiment can make any progress without (often taken-for-granted) interpretations of the situation, as perceived by the experimental subjects, and interpretations of their actions. Furthermore, I would argue that once this interpretive dimension is present, a value-critical element is present as well.

I conclude that any objection to looking at Kierkegaard as a Christian psychologist on the grounds that psychology is limited to empirical research and that Kierkegaard didn't do such research is misguided. If, as I have yet to show, Kierkegaard has valuable things to teach Christian psychologists in interpreting and critically reflecting on human behavior, then the most that could legitimately be said in criticism is that he does not provide a well-rounded role model for Christian psychologists because the empirical aspect of his work is underdeveloped. This is a criticism that I will concede at the outset. I hope that one of the results of this work will be the stimulation of empirical research that remedies this gap and puts some of Kierkegaard's insights to the test of observation.

Meaning and Interpretation in Psychology: The Role of Subjectivity

Interpretation is a key element in all psychology because human activity is constituted by meaning.[10] Although there are simple biological reflexes and (probably) some vestigial biological instincts, the preponderance of human behavior is meaningful. What a person is doing at a particular time is dependent on the meaning of that activity. The same bodily movement may be many different actions; the same action may be carried out by many bodily movements. A woman who raises her arm may be voting, doing aerobic exercise, striving for recognition, or just stretching to wake herself. The same woman may vote by marking a piece of paper, pulling a lever, uttering a word, standing, or shouting.

To say that action is constituted by meaning is not to say that we are always thinking about that meaning. Nor does it mean that we are always clear about the meaning of our actions, because we are often confused or even ignorant about what we are doing. But we are usually aware of what we are doing, and if you ask someone what he is about, he can usually tell you.

If this view of human activity is correct, then observing human behavior is a more complex procedure than might at first be imagined. To see what someone is doing, we must do more than see the bodily movements; we must understand the meaning of those movements. Of course, in the case of familiar behavior in our own culture, we do this all the time with no particular difficulties; that is why the empiricist attempt to minimize the importance of interpretation is as successful as it is. Nevertheless, though no conscious process of interpretation goes on in such cases, observing human behavior still involves something like an interpretive judgment. This becomes transparent as soon as we turn to bizarre behavior in our own culture or look at an alien culture.

How are we able to make these interpretive judgments? There is nothing magical about it; it is done through ordinary experience and requires no special "intuition." In growing up in a culture we learn that in certain contexts certain kinds of behavior usually have a particular meaning. One problem this raises is that the interpretive judgments we make depend on others we have already made. This is often called "the hermeneutical circle." I see that someone is voting at a committee meeting because I know that when people raise their hands at such a meeting at a particular time, the act is an act of voting. But of course my ability to recognize the act of voting presupposes that I have already recognized the meeting as a committee meeting and that I understand the meaning of the chairman's request that all who are in favor of the motion will please raise their hands. How do we break into this hermeneutical circle? We do so by having learned how to live as a part of a human community.

It is important to note that we learn these things not simply by making observations; we could not in fact make any observations if we could not already make some judgments of this sort. We learn these things in the process of learning how to act ourselves, in the process of becoming a part of the culture. To use Kierkegaard's language, we learn them in the course of learning how to exist. Later, to the extent that we are able to understand people who are very different from ourselves—particularly those from very different cultures— we do so by imaginatively extending our world, trying to understand what it would be like to be those other someones.

It follows from this that there are real limitations in our ability to understand other people's behavior. A human action is a possible way of being, and to the extent that I do not understand this way of being, I do not understand the action, even if I can successfully stick a label on it. Imagine that an extraterrestrial who had no acquaintance with religion were to visit earth and observe a group of Muslims in their daily prayers. He might be able to coin a word for this activity (perhaps he will call it "daily body prostration") and consist- ently apply that word, but he will hardly understand the behavior without understanding a host of other things, such as God, relationship to God, faith, devotion, obedience, and authority. And he cannot understand these things without getting some feel for what it is like to be religious. Of course he does not actually have to be religious, but he must at least be able to enter the religious life in his imagination.

All this implies that there is a profound difference between observing events in the nonhuman natural world and observing human behavior. In the case of the nonhuman world we can only observe things by applying concepts to them, and these concepts have meaning as well. But we clearly under- stand that the objects we observe exist independently of these meanings. Lightning was lightning long before there was any human concept of lightning. But prayer can be prayer only when people have something like a concept of prayer. Here the meaning of the event is essential to the reality of the event in a way that is not the case for the nonhuman world.

The upshot of all this is that in regard to human behavior, our own existence may be a crucial factor in our ability to observe other people's behavior accurately. My ability to recognize moral behavior may depend on the extent to which I have actually entered the moral life myself, or at least may depend on my ability to understand what it would be like to do so.

For human actions, in a much more profound sense than for other natural events, there are no immaculate perceptions. The observer has a critical contribution to make to the observation; her own skills, attitudes, values, and experiences heavily shape how she sees and what she sees. Kierkegaard perceived this very clearly and therefore emphasizes the role of the subjective participation of the observer.

> What one sees depends on how one sees. This is because all observation is not merely a receiving, a discovery, but also a creation, and to the extent that it is this latter, the decisive factor becomes how the observer himself is. . . . To the extent that the object of the observation is part of the external world, the condition of the observer is a matter of indifference, or, rather, that which is essential to the observation does not concern his deeper being. On the other hand, the more the object of observation belongs to the world of spirit, the more important is the state of the innermost being of the observer.[11]

This means that the condition of the observer must not be seen simply as a possible set of biases that will distort the observations. Such bias is indeed possible, but at times the condition of the observer is an essential, enabling condition that allows the true meaning of the behavior to be revealed.

Examples of this sort are not hard to find. All of us are acquainted with reductionistic accounts of the religious life offered by people with no understanding of the meaning of the religious life. Or we think of the cynical, suspicious reporter who cannot accept the devotion and altruism of the saint. The paranoid who perceives the friendly attempts of others to help him as sinister is simply an extreme example of the way personal qualities may distort one's experience of others; the often unnoticed flip side of this is that just as some qualities may distort or bias observation, so others may be necessary to grasp them in their fullness or wholeness.

We can see immediately, then, that psychology in a Kierkegaardian mode puts a good deal of emphasis on the personal qualities of the psychologist. To some degree this Kierkegaardian insight is recognized in contemporary psychology, particularly in clinical training programs that stress the need for the therapist to undergo therapy. But this recognition is in tension with the often-prevailing model of scientist-practitioner, which does not pay a lot of attention to the moral and spiritual character of the scientist.

Kierkegaard's Method of Critical Introspection and Observation

Kierkegaard's primary goal as a psychologist is to understand meanings as human life possibilities. What methods does he use to do this? He does observe the lives of people around him; indeed, he is an extremely keen observer. However, the primary sources of his insights are his introspective experience and reflections on his own life. The term "introspection" raises many red flags to psychologists. It carries with it the baggage of the discredited attempts by Titchener and Wundt to establish scientific psychology through trained, introspective observers.

However, the merits and demerits of the introspective methods of Wundt and Titchener are completely irrelevant to what Kierkegaard is doing. They used introspection as a source of knowledge about psychological events or occurrences. I think it is correct to claim that when used in this way, introspection—while not without value—is subject to severe limitations. However, this is not at all what Kierkegaard is doing. He uses introspection, not to discover what events are occurring right now inside his head, but to understand meanings, possible ways of being. His method is more properly described as recollection than introspection, since his focus is on understanding patterns of action that have a history and not on recording contemporaneous events.

We have already seen that interpretation is an element in all psychological observation of meaningful human behavior. For this task, introspection or critical recollection in Kierkegaard's sense is not only a valid method; it is really the only possible method. Understanding of meanings is possible only through participation in human life; grasping of new meanings is possible only through reflection on that participation.

Nor is Kierkegaard's method alien to psychology as it is

practiced today. Despite the appearance of greater scientific objectivity that the secular character of the field makes possible, when we actually look at clinical theories we see that almost all the significant ones have important roots in the case-study method that relies very heavily on interpretation. Theories that stem from the psychodynamic tradition often are grounded in a self-analysis which closely parallels Kierkegaard's method. The one apparent exception is cognitive behavioral therapy, which claims to rely on "scientific" results. I believe, however, that even in this case interpretation plays a major role in theory development and selection.

One might think that the possible meanings of human actions would be infinite, and in a sense this is completely correct. We could not begin to catalog all the possible types of human actions and their many possible meanings. However, the meaning of a particular action is usually best understood as part of a larger context, the life story of the individual. I go to the store to buy a loaf of bread. This act takes on meaning in the context of my need to make lunch for my children. My attempts to love and care for my children take on meaning in the context of my decisions to marry and have children, and those decisions in turn reflect larger decisions about the meaning and purpose of life.

What Kierkegaard really wants to do is to understand those larger contexts, to try to see how the myriad choices and activities of people can be understood as attempts to realize various ideals of life. He believed that the number of possible ideal lives is not at all infinite; the tremendously varied characters of actual lives can usefully be viewed as attempts to realize one or more of a relatively small number of life ideals. These possibilities he saw not only as possibilities that he could see himself living out, but as actually realized in the lives of people around him.

Many of the most significant human possibilities come to expression in representative figures or archetypes, often to be found in literary form. Thus, for Christian culture Kierkegaard saw particular significance in the figures of Don Juan, Faust, and Ahasuerus (the Wandering Jew), who embody respectively the possibilities of sensuousness, doubt, and despair as ultimate life meanings. Equally significant on the positive side of the ledger are biblical figures such as Abraham, Job, and Mary in helping us to clarify the life of faith and the meanings of actions within such a life.

It is obvious that Kierkegaard's descriptions of meaningful life-possibilities are not value-free, but this is not really an objection. As soon as meanings are taken seriously, a value-free perspective becomes impossible. Kierkegaard's descriptions are not value-free, because he believes that human beings are created in such a way that certain sets of possibilities lead to their flourishing, while others lead to spiritual death.

Kierkegaard's Interpretive Framework

Granted that his psychology aims at understanding ideal life-possibilities and emphasizes the crucial role played by the personal qualities of the observer, what particular interpretive framework does Kierkegaard bring to bear on human life? To some degree, the rest of this book is designed to answer this question. Nevertheless, some preliminary orientation is necessary.

Kierkegaard's interpretive framework is consciously Christian. It is certainly not the only Christian framework that could be brought to bear on the phenomena. Moreover, the non-Christian would recognize much of it as correct—which is what we would hope to be the case if Christianity is true. Nevertheless, Kierkegaard's psychology is not only Christian in its intent. (We saw in chapter 1 that one of his central purposes in doing psychology is to assist the missionary whose call is to "Christendom.") It is also Christian in that the major themes and insights he brings to bear on human life are derived from his Christian beliefs and personal Christian experiences.

Any distinctively Christian approach to psychology will in some way or other deal with the great Christian themes of creation, fall, and redemption, and Kierkegaard's thought is no exception. For him, the concept of creation implies that human beings are primarily spiritual creatures. Though humans are bodily creatures, they do not live by bread alone; they are bodily spirits. In the next chapter we will try to understand how Kierkegaard works out his conception of human beings as spirit. To say that human beings are spirit is to say that they were created to enjoy a relationship with God and can only be themselves through such a relationship.

Human sinfulness appears in Kierkegaard's thought primarily in the phenomenon of self-deception. Though made for a relation with God, humans have rebelled against him. For this reason, human beings are constantly resisting their own true happiness and fighting against their own best interests. This struggle is impossible without massive self-ignorance and self-deception, and Kierkegaard believes that is precisely what an honest look at the human condition reveals. His Christian psychology thus turns out to be a form of depth psychology in which people's conscious awareness is often a surface awareness that is very far from the truth. We will explore this non-Freudian depth psychology in chapters 4 through 6.

Both our spiritual character and our sinfulness are illuminated by a look at the process of human growth and development. Kierkegaard has a developmental theory that is attuned both to what might be called healthy development and to the pervasive effects of sin; we will examine this theory in chapter 7. Because of sin, the process of human development must be seen not only as development, but as recovery. Therefore, discussions of growth must be coupled with discussions of human redemption in Christ.

In chapter 8 I will try to distill lessons from this framework for the Christian who is seeking to help a fellow human being move toward greater wholeness. Here Kierkegaard offers, to both the professional and the layperson, the concept of the maieutic healer. Such a healer is aware of the limits of his ability to help another, imposed by his own finitude and by the other's freedom, but nonetheless he has a sense of how a person can, with God's help, contribute to the flourishing of another.

In the concluding chapter I will try to show the value of Kierkegaard's distinctively Christian approach to psychological questions for applied psychology. Perhaps our fictional Dr. John can meet some of Kirk's concerns without compromising his integrity as a psychologist.

Notes

1. See my *Preserving the Person* (Downers Grove, Ill.: InterVarsity Press, 1977; Grand Rapids; Baker, 1982) for a discussion of this category.

2. Søren Kierkegaard, *The Sickness unto Death*, ed. and trans. Howard V. Hong and Edna H. Hong (Princeton: Princeton University Press, 1980), 5. Though I always supply pagination from the English edition for the reader's convenience, the translations used are sometimes my own. Subsequent page references in parentheses in the text all refer to *The Sickness unto Death*.

3. I believe that the pseudonymn Anti-Climacus holds views identical to Kierkegaard's own and that the pseudonym was added simply because Kierkegaard did not feel he personally measured up to the rigorous Christian standards employed by Anti-Climacus. He wished therefore to direct the book to himself as well as other readers and for this purpose used a pseudonymous "ideal Christian." Since the beliefs of Kierkegaard and Anti-Climacus are therefore the same, I will in the future refer merely to Kierkegaard. For a discussion of Kierkegaard's use of pseudonyms and his purposes in doing so, see chapter 7.

4. For a careful review of the current status of philosophy of science, see Del Ratzsch, *Philosophy of Science* (Downers Grove, Ill.: InterVarsity Press, 1986). Ratzsch carefully states the traditional or standard empiricist view of science, explains the attack on the view that originated in the work of Thomas Kuhn, and develops a sane perspective that takes account of the role values and presuppositions play in science, without plunging into the relativism of Kuhn.

5. See James D. Foster and Mark F. Ledbetter, "Christian Anti-Psychology and the Scientific Method," *Journal of Psychology and Theology* 15, no. 1 (1987): 10–18.

6. See my *Wisdom and Humanness in Psychology: Prospects for a Christian Approach* (Grand Rapids: Baker, 1989).

7. See again *Wisdom and Humanness in Psychology*, especially chapter 2. This chapter is in turn indebted to a book by David Braybrooke, *Philosophy of Social Science* (Englewood Cliffs, N.J.: Prentice-Hall, 1987). Braybrooke calls these three dimensions the naturalistic side, the interpretative side, and the critical side of social science. He does not specifically apply his views to psychology, as I do, and I disagree with him about several significant issues in his characterizations of three dimensions. Nevertheless, the thesis I defend in this section is substantially similar to his.

8. For a detailed version of this argument see chapter 3 of *Wisdom and Humanness in Psychology*.

9. See Stanley Milgram, "Behavioral Study of Obedience," *Journal of Abnormal and Social Psychology* 67 (1963): 371–78.

10. See chapter 3 of *Wisdom and Humanness in Psychology*.

11. Søren Kierkegaard, *Edifying Discourses*, vol. 1 (Minneapolis: Augsburg Publishing House, 1943), 67.

Human Beings
as Spiritual Creatures

Kierkegaard's fundamental insight into the human person is that people are spiritual creatures. This concept is one mark of a distinctively Christian psychology, and it is a mark that clearly differentiates Kierkegaard's thought from the vast majority of twentieth-century psychological theories.

It is not easy to gain a clear understanding of what Kierkegaard means when he says, as he does in *The Sickness unto Death*, that "a human being is spirit." The concept of spirit and spirituality is clouded by many misleading associations and misconceptions. So we must begin by saying what spirituality is not.

First, to be spirit is not to be a ghost residing in a body. To some Christians, talk of spirit is talk of a ghostly entity that dwells somewhere in the body and is loosely attached to it. The truth this misleading image tries to capture is that human beings are not purely physical creatures; we are not understandable in purely physical terms, and the essential core of our being is capable of being reinvested in radically different bodies. This is an essential teaching of the church—one which Kierkegaard wholeheartedly accepted and one in which his own confidence in the face of death was surely rooted. However, it is important to see that spirit is something I myself am; it is not an entity residing in me.

Once the image of the ghost in the machine is rejected,

we are free to acknowledge the full significance of the body to my spirituality. The body is more than a house in which my spirit lives (although the apostle Paul uses the metaphor of a tent to convey the truth that my present body is not essential to my personhood.) The body is the form of my spirituality, the way I exist as a spiritual being. Human beings are embodied spirits, and a recognition of their spiritual character by no means entails that the body is insignificant to their identity.

A second misleading image of spirituality is to see spiritual existence as simply indwelling by God's Spirit. Here the model for spiritual existence is, I think, something like demon possession, odd as that may seem. In a case of demon possession, a supernatural entity enters a person's body and controls or influences his actions. Many Christians, without perhaps quite realizing it, think of spiritual existence as something like this, except that they replace the demon with the Spirit of God. Someone who is employing this model may think of a spiritual person as one who makes choices on the basis of mystical inner promptings ("the leading of the Spirit") rather than thinking things through rationally.

I certainly affirm that the Spirit of God indwells the believer, and I wholeheartedly believe that God can speak to the individual and offer special guidance for crucial decisions. There are two problems with understanding spirituality merely as indwelling, however.

First, this understanding obscures an important truth: spirituality must be understood as both a descriptive and a normative term. It is both ontological and ethical, connected to what I am and to what I must become. Spirituality is partly something to strive for. Christians are commanded to become and to live as spiritual beings. But spirituality is also an aspect of our created humanness; humans beings have no choice but to be spiritual.

To focus on spirituality as indwelling is to focus solely on its normative aspect, which causes us to miss or de-emphasize the important truth that humans, though made from dust, were made to commune with God and therefore have a spiritual destiny. We are all in one sense spiritual beings, whether or not we experience God's indwelling.

The second problem with the indwelling-as-possession

model is that it overemphasizes the normative character of spirituality. It is quite right to think of spirituality as a condition in which the individual is dependent on God and therefore sensitive to God's leading, and it is true that God sometimes leads through inner feelings that may not be explained fully by reason. However, it is quite wrong to see this as the only way or even the main way that Christians are led by the Spirit of God. Spiritual guidance is also—in fact, mainly—gained through being tuned to God's Word. As the spirit illumines our hearts and teaches us more about God's character and doings, our understanding of the nature of God's kingdom increases and our ability to make wise, godly decisions likewise increases. Living spiritually, therefore, is not to be identified with a state in which the mind is depreciated.

Even in cases where the Spirit of God prompts the person through mystical inner feelings, there is a big difference between God's indwelling and demonic possession. A demon possesses a person as an alien being, so the person's normal human capacities are thwarted or overridden. God dwells within his children to help them become the kind of people he wants them to be—their true selves. Thus God's actions within them are aimed at developing and fostering their capacities.

Spirituality as Relational Being

I have said something about what spirit is not, so now we must ask, what is it? Kierkegaard's answer to this question is legendary in its difficulty and obscurity:

> A human being is spirit. But what is spirit? Spirit is the self. But what is the self? The self is a relation that relates itself to itself or is the relation's relating itself to itself in the relation; the self is not the relation but is the relation's relating itself to itself (p. 13).[1]

This is more than a mouthful, but I believe that if it is rightly analyzed, there is genuine wisdom here.

We can begin by noting the most obvious implication of the passage: whatever else spirit is, it is relational. Spirit is a complicated sort of being. One cannot understand a spiritual being *all by itself* as a simple entity; its being is constituted by its relations.

The passage I have just quoted refers only to a special kind of relation—the relation of the self to itself. Kierkegaard does not intend to claim that human beings can be understood in isolation from their relation to other selves. In a passage that closely follows this one, he staunchly maintains that we can only understand the relationship of a self to itself in the light of the relationship of self to others: "The human self is . . . a relation that relates itself to itself and in relating itself to itself relates itself to another" (pp. 13–14).

So the emphasis on the relation of the self to itself is not a claim that the self can be understood in isolation. Rather, even when we focus on the individual self, we find not a simple entity, but a complex relationship. As spiritual beings, humans are relational right down to the core, even on the "inside," so to speak.

Several things follow from this relational view of personhood. First, if Kierkegaard is correct, then in our dialogue between Dr. John and Kirk in chapter 2, Kirk is quite justified in his suspicion that any account of personhood that leaves God out of the picture will be seriously deficient. If human beings are spirit, if to be spirit is to be relational, and if the relation to God as Creator is the most basic relationship humans have, then it seems that the God-relation cannot be a peripheral, add-on fact about human beings.

The second implication of Kierkegaard's relational view stems from the fact that God is the ultimate relater. Many contemporary thinkers would agree with Kierkegaard that personhood is relational in character, but they think that the essential relations are purely temporal. People are the products of human societies. On this view, a "person" is ultimately whatever we regard as a person, and the personhood of those who do not have significant social roles to play is very much in doubt.

We shall see that Kierkegaard also regards human relations as important in the formation of the self. However, the relation to God is fundamental, and because of that relation there is a sense in which our being as spiritual creatures can be relational, yet substantial too. Every human being has a relationship to God the Creator, on whom our ultimate status as persons depends. The aged, the sick, and the unborn all have status in God's eyes, even if they presently lack the capacity for human social interaction that our culture regards as the essence of personhood. So for Kierkegaard (and this theme will be developed later), the term "person" describes both something I *am*, by virtue of God's creative activity, and something I must *become*, in and through my relations with God and other people.

Substitutes for the God-Relationship

The final implication of Kierkegaard's relational view of spirituality that I wish to discuss is that spirituality can take many forms and can have various qualities. If my being as spirit is constituted by relationships, then the nature of those relationships will determine the nature of my being. What I relate to and the character of those relations shape my identity.

We have already stressed that the ultimate "what" for all human beings is God, in whom we truly "live and move and have our being." However, God does not unilaterally determine the nature of human persons; he has created us as free and responsible beings. As Kierkegaard says in *The Sickness Unto Death*, "God, who constituted man a relation, releases it from his hand, as it were" (p. 16). Notice that there is no true independence from God. God does not really let the relationship "go out of his hand," but he endows humans with the freedom to choose, so that the relation goes out of his hands "as it were."

This freedom does not diminish humans as relational beings; nor do they cease to have a relation to God. Rather, the consequence is that they may cease to relate consciously to God, forming their selves in relation to what is less than God.

> And what infinite reality the self gains by being conscious of existing before God, by becoming a human self whose criterion is God! A cattleman who (if this were possible) is a self directly before his cattle is a very low self, and, similarly, a master who is a self directly before his slaves is actually no self—for in both cases a criterion is lacking. The child who previously has had only his parents as a criterion becomes a self as an adult by

getting the state as a criterion, but what an infinite accent falls
on the self by having God as the criterion! (p. 79)

Here Kierkegaard deepens our understanding of the
relational character of the self. By a "criterion" he means that
by which a self measures itself. To be a self is to be a being
who is striving toward a certain ideal; that ideal provides the
"measure" or "criterion" for the self. For human selves, at
least, this measure is derived from the conscious relationships
that have formed the self.

Psychologists today recognize the importance of human
relationships in forming the identity of the self, and in this
quotation it can be seen that Kierkegaard agrees with them.
There is a natural progression as the identity of the child is
formed first through the relation to the parents, then to society
in general, and finally to God. In each case the relation
provides an ideal of the self that serves as a measure for it.

It is not, of course, pathological for the child, who is only
in the process of becoming a self in the deepest sense, to
ground her identity in her parents, or the older child to ground
her identity in broader social roles and expectations. Such
relations are crucial in forming what I would term the "pre-
self" (not a Kierkegaardian term), the self I am when I am not
yet a self in the decisive sense. The pre-self is the self that has
been produced by my heredity and environment prior to my
becoming aware of my responsibility to become the self I
should be. The fact is that when I become conscious of my
responsibility to decide who I should be, I am already a self of
sorts, and this self has been formed through early experience
with others.

Kierkegaard believes that the pre-self is not a self in the
decisive sense because it lacks a relation to God. Genuine
selfhood requires that I stand before God, accepting the self I
am as a gift from God and the self I should become as a task
God has set for me. People who lack such a relation fail to be
selves in the most decisive sense. In the young child this lack
is not pathological and is to be expected. However, in adults
the attempt to ground the self in what is less than God is
pathological. This does not mean that the adult should not
continue to have relations with other human selves that help

to define his identity. To use Kierkegaard's example, the cattleman is a cattleman and that is part of his identity. It is rather that those relations must not exhaust one's identity. The cattleman must always be more than just a cattleman.

A person who thinks of himself as a self only through his superiority to the cattle he tends is actually not a self at all; one might say his standards are too low. Similarly, a person whose selfhood is completely grounded in his perceived superiority to the slaves he owns fails to be a self. This is so, not because he is not related to other selves—his slaves are persons—but because in regarding the slaves as slaves, the owner does not regard them as genuine selves. Thus his measure is a defective one, and this infects his own self-conception.

We are, of course, all too familiar with the phenomenon Kierkegaard addresses here. The most common pathological way in which humans ground their identity in what is less than God is through comparison. All of us, though some more than others, compare ourselves with other people, and it is all too common for people's identity to rest on their similarity to the group they belong to and their perceived superiority to someone who is different. The racist whose identity is bound up with the color of his skin is one obvious example of this tendency. Kierkegaard knows that many human selves are formed in this way, but a self that only has other human beings as its measure can never be secure. Genuine selfhood requires that the self "stand before God."

More on this will follow. For now we must simply see that though God is the actual ground of all selfhood, the self develops as it relates to other finite beings. This is not in itself pathological, but it becomes so when the adult refuses to recognize the God who is the ground of genuine selfhood and attempts to build his identity solely on what is less than God.

In this we see once more the blend of the descriptive and the normative, the ontological and the ethical, in Kierkegaard's view of the self. The self is both something a human being is and something a human being must become. A relationship to God is in one sense inescapable; in another it is a task. However, the structure of the self is always formed in relation to some ideal. The self that lacks God as conscious ideal will reflect the defective ideal that has replaced God. The results can be seen in the person whose identity is bound up with gaining more power than others in the company, or with having a fancier car than the neighbors, or with more social prestige than others. The quality of a self reflects the particular nature of the individual's ideal self, and the nature of that ideal self is always relationally determined.

Thus, insofar as spirituality is relational in character, there are different kinds of spirituality. There is genuine spirituality, and there are counterfeit forms of it. Human beings form themselves in relation to the spirit of God but also in relation to the spirits of this fallen world. This does not mean that relations to other finite selves are pathological. They become so only when they become the ultimate basis of the self, a substitute for the God-relation.

The Incongruous Components of Human Selfhood

It is time to return to the puzzling description of the self from which we started. What does it mean to say that the self is "a relation which relates itself to itself"? We have seen that the self is fundamentally relational, that the ultimate relater is always God, though human selves are all too often formed in conscious relation to what is less than God. But what is the nature of the self that is thus formed through relations to others?

That question divides itself into two others. First, what is this internal relation that makes up the self? Second, what does it mean to say that this relation is in turn relational, that it "relates itself to itself?"

The first question is answered straightforwardly by Kierkegaard. The relation that composes human selfhood is described as a "synthesis." "A human being is a synthesis of the infinite and the finite, of the temporal and eternal, of freedom and necessity" (p. 13).

That human beings are made up of contrasting or even incongruous elements is not exactly news, but the point is so basic that its significance is likely to be missed. Socrates is reported to have wondered whether he was more like a monster or a god. Pascal expressed the idea more eloquently than anyone else:

> What kind of freak then is man? How novel, how monstrous, how chaotic, how paradoxical, how prodigious! Judge of all things, feeble earthworm, repository of truth, sink of doubt and error, glory and refuse of the universe![2]

Human beings are capable of the grandest plans and schemes, noble and heroic actions, beautiful and moving poetry, intricate and complex scientific knowledge. But these same human beings can behave in the most spiteful way if they lose a little sleep, and they exhibit the grossest selfishness in competing for a bigger piece of pie. They are continually at the mercy of conditions largely beyond their control—a fire at the wrong place and time, and their lives are snuffed out like a candle.

Kierkegaard sums up this fundamental incongruity in the terms "infinite" and "finite," "eternal" and "temporal," "freedom and necessity." Infinity, eternity, and freedom focus on what we might call the *expansive* pole of the synthesis. Fundamentally, it is the power of consciousness that underlies this aspect of the self. Consciousness gives us the power to imagine what does not exist; in our imagination we can conceive scientific theories that have not yet been established, create poetic imagery that has never been voiced, envision actions that have never been carried through, and hope to become persons with a character that differs greatly from our actual character.

This expansive, infinitizing pole is hardly the whole story, however. The *limiting*, finite side of the self comes clearly into view when I reflect on my bodily character. Because I am a physical being, I have only a limited number and range of experiences. The body informs me that I have not chosen to be born at all and that I did not choose to be born to my particular parents at a particular place. My bodily character highlights the precariousness of my being, my constant dependence on conditions that I try to control with varying degrees of success.

As Kierkegaard sees it, the task of human selfhood is not to minimize either of these incongruous elements. It is to synthesize them, to unify what appears to be contradictory. The task is to exercise creatively the freedom that is made possible by consciousness, but to do this within the concrete limitations of my actual situation. A person who cannot dream, who has no ideals or goals, is not fully human. But a person who dreams grand dreams, yet never takes a concrete step toward making them real because they have no relation to the particular circumstances of his life, is equally inhuman.

The Significance of Self-Consciousness

If we see the human self merely as a synthesis of incongruous elements, we still do not see it as self, according to Kierkegaard. For the self is not just a relation, but a "self-relating relation." What does this mean? How can I have a relationship to my self?

For the self to have a relationship to itself, there must obviously be a duality of sorts in the self. There is the self to which I am relating and there is the self that is doing the relating. This puzzling concept of the dual self corresponds exactly to our experience. I continually experience myself both as object and as subject. I think about what I have become, what I have done, what I feel, what I hope. But there is also the elusive "I" that is thinking about this first "I."

Humans do not only have consciousness, which is what makes the synthesis of incongruous elements possible. They also possess self-consciousness, which means that the synthesis is not a static, completed object, but a dynamic process. Furthermore, the process is one I have some hand in shaping. The power of self-consciousness means that I am always in some sense "outside myself." Or, to be more exact, I am a never-finished process of relating myself to self. There is the self that I have become, and there is the self that I project myself as becoming. I am in the process of moving from one to the other.

This becomes clearer if we reflect on the way humans experience time. For human selves, time is "tensed time." We experience time not only as a uniform succession of moments, but also as qualitatively distinct phases of past, present, and future. For Kierkegaard this structure reflects the structure of the self. Without self-consciousness time would lack these "tensed" qualities. The past encompasses the self as a determinate object of consciousness, what I have become. The future represents open possibilities, what I could become. The present is the moment in which I attempt to unite the two, to project my past into a future. This is possible because of self-consciousness, the power to step back and look at my self.

We could express this paradoxically by saying that a self is always more than itself. A self is essentially a self-transcending being that outruns what it is in the sense of what it has become. But it is truer to say that what a self is reflects what it will become as much as what it has become. My identity is defined by my goals as well as by my achievements.

Relating to Self by Relating to God

Kierkegaard's view of the self is in some respects similar to that of other "existential psychologies." He emphasizes that the self is not merely an object to be studied, but a subject, which means it is a dynamic, unfolding process. As self-conscious beings we can control the process to some degree. Thus a self is both something I am and something I must choose to become, as I take responsibility for my life.

At this point, however, Kierkegaard diverges sharply from secular existentialists. Two alternatives are posed: "Such a relation that relates itself to itself, a self, must either have established itself or have been established by another." In other words, the self is either autonomous or dependent on another for its being. Considering Kierkegaard's view of the self as relational, there can be no doubt as to which view he holds. The human self is always grounded in a higher power. "The human self is such a derived, established relation, a relation that relates itself to itself and in relating itself to itself relates itself to another."

We have noted already that the "other" to which the self must relate is fundamentally God, who is the ontological foundation of the self. However, we saw that as the self actually develops, it consciously relates to what is less than God. In the pre-self of the child this is natural and normal. However, when the mature self attempts to base itself solely on these relations, they become God-substitutes. Whether I relate to God or a God-substitute, I am not autonomous; I relate to myself by relating to something that transcends myself.

As created substances, human beings are always related to God. The relation is not always a self-conscious one, however, and insofar as a person is something I must become, I can base my self on something less than God. I am never completely self-sufficient, and insofar as I do relate to something less than God, my autonomy is decreased rather than increased. This is because the self always reflects the status of its relational ideal. The person who is content to be a self before cattle, or simply in relation to other people he may be superior to in some ways, is less of a self than the one who stands before God. Kierkegaard says, "What an infinite accent falls on the self by having God as the criterion" (p. 79).

The secular existentialist typically sees the self as totally autonomous: I must create myself by my choices. Kierkegaard sees things very differently. The self was created by God, and therefore the self I can choose to be or not to be is in one sense given to me. And even the self which (futilely, ultimately) flees the God-relationship is not truly autonomous. I can only be myself by a relation to that ideal outside myself which has formed the self. Human freedom is always limited and finite.

All this can be seen more clearly by looking at the ways human beings fail to be a self. If I were truly autonomous, the only genuine way of failing to be a self would be to fail to exercise my freedom and choose.

From Kierkegaard's point of view, however, there are two ways of failing to be a self. This failure he calls "despair," and we will analyze this in chapters 4 through 6. Here we will merely note that this despair takes two forms: the *despair of weakness* and the *despair of defiance*. The despair of weakness is a failure to choose, to become the self God has created me to be. The despair of defiance is grounded in the attempt to become autonomous, to be the self I choose to be. The latter form is, for the secular existentialist, genuine and authentic selfhood. For Kierkegaard it represents a tragic failure.

Similarly, the conscious dependence on God that the secular existentialist sees as inauthentic selfhood, or running away from freedom, Kierkegaard sees as providing true selfhood and true freedom. God had an ideal in view when he created human beings, and he has an ideal for me as well.

In a famous essay, Jean-Paul Sartre defined existentialism

as the view that in the case of human beings, "existence precedes essence." What he meant is that there is no normative ideal for human beings. What we are is completely up to us. We create ourselves through our choices, and no choice can be considered right or wrong in any objective sense.

In this sense of the term Kierkegaard is obviously not an existentialist, because he clearly believes that human beings have an essence. Unlike Sartre, he does not view this fact as a threat to our freedom or dignity, because he sees freedom as part of our created essence. God created humans to be responsible choosers. The choices are not indifferent; to choose to turn away from God and his ways is to choose not to become my true self. However, the fact that this true self is given, and not invented by me out of nothing, does not negate my freedom. It is, in fact, what makes my freedom meaningful. The freedom Sartre believes humans possess seems more absolute, but actually it makes all choices arbitrary and meaningless. There can be no concern for making good choices unless some choices are really good.

The ideal self God intends me to be is therefore not incompatible with freedom; it includes freedom as an essential element. Furthermore, it does not preclude individuality and creativity. There are universal ideals that all humans should recognize, such as love and justice. However, it is up to me to strive creatively to actualize these ideals in the unique and particular circumstances in which God has placed me. Another ideal is that humans should strive to recognize and develop the unique gifts and talents God has granted them. As Kierkegaard puts it, every person has, from God's point of view, a unique name (pp. 33–34). God knows me as an individual and wants me to have the courage to become the unique person he created me to be. "Every human being is primitively intended to be a self, destined to become himself, and as such every self certainly is angular, but that only means that it is to be ground into shape, not that it is to be ground down smooth, not that it is utterly to abandon being itself out of fear of men" (p. 33).

Kierkegaard is often criticized as an individualist. We have seen that this charge is in one sense unjustified. Kierkegaard has a thoroughly relational view of the self: we can only be a self in relation to others. However, there is a legitimate kind of individualism. For Kierkegaard, God created each person and loves each one individually, not only as part of a collective. Each person has the privilege and the responsibility of standing before God as an individual. This is one's privilege as a spiritual creature.

We have said little about spirituality in terms of its implications for life after death. For Kierkegaard, spirituality does not involve only a spiritual "part" that can survive death. But because we are fundamentally spiritual beings, we have an eternal destiny. This is evident in that despair, that loss of selfhood which is "the sickness unto death," does not lead to death. "Socrates proved the immortality of the soul from the fact that sickness of the soul (sin) does not consume it as sickness of the body consumes the body. Similarly, the eternal in a person can be proved by the fact that despair cannot consume his self" (p. 21).

I do not think Kierkegaard means that we can literally prove humans are immortal merely by observing that despair does not truly lead to extinction of selfhood. Rather, I think the nature of despair can be seen as a clue or pointer to our true nature or identity. Just as Socrates saw immortality in the fact that a damaged soul—a soul suffering from sin—continues to be, so Kierkegaard sees a clue to the soul's immortality in the fact that a tormented soul—a soul that wills its own nothingness—continues to be. The fact that the sick self cannot really destroy itself indicates that it still stands before God and is addressed by God. As spiritual beings, humans are eternal, not in themselves, but because of their relation to God. "To have a self, to be a self, is the greatest concession . . . given to man, but it is eternity's claim upon him" (p. 21).

Notes

1. The reader is reminded that the page numbers in parentheses all refer to *The Sickness unto Death*.

2. Blaise Pascal, *Pensées*, trans. A. J. Krailsheimer (New York: Penguin, 1966), 64.

CHAPTER 4

Kierkegaard's Depth Psychology I: Sin, Anxiety, and Despair

As a Christian psychologist Kierkegaard knows that human beings are not only spiritual beings, but are also spiritually dead. The heart of his discussion of concrete forms of human life focuses on sin.

Kierkegaard's understanding of sin follows directly from his understanding of persons as dependent on God. God has created each of us to be unique individuals, and we can only be so by consciously relating to God. Sin, for Kierkegaard, is a break in the God-relationship, a rebellious, prideful attempt by human beings to be autonomous. This rebellion expresses itself psychologically as despair. "Sin is: *before God, or with the conception of God, in despair not to will to be oneself, or in despair to will to be oneself*" (p. 77). We will explore several aspects of this definition later, but for now we can see its major thrust now by contrasting it with the opposite of sin: faith. "Faith is: that the self in being itself and in willing to be itself rests transparently in God" (p. 82).

A superficial view—often passed off as Christian—equates sin with particular acts of wrongdoing. The error in this view is that it loses sight of sin as a condition or state. The problem is not in the assertion that some acts are sins; it is the failure to see that the origin of sinful deeds lies in an underlying attitude of prideful autonomy over against God. The failure to see this leads straight to Pharisaism, because it obscures the fact that sin often comes disguised as virtuous behavior. Such behavior can be a particularly insidious—and effective—way of rebelling against God, of failing to be the individual God has created me to become. As we shall see, I can be a "good" person and a social conformist—someone who unthinkingly conforms to established social practices—with no thought ultimately of any responsibility for becoming what I should be. Alternatively, "being good" can be a form of defiance, a way of telling God that I need no help to become what I should be.

Kierkegaard makes this point by identifying the opposite of sin not as virtue (using this term in a somewhat unusual way), but faith. Faith is a matter of being oneself before God or, put more actively, being willing to be oneself while resting transparently in God. Of course, these are not two distinct tasks. I don't have to be myself first and then relate properly to God. Rather, I become myself by relating properly to him. Given the relational character of Kierkegaard's "self," there is no other way of being a self than by relating to another, and there is no way to be my genuine self than by relating to God.

The contrast of faith with virtue is a bit surprising since many Christians would insist that faith is a virtue—indeed, along with love and hope a specifically Christian virtue. It is clear here that by "virtue" Kierkegaard means something like "behavior that is morally acceptable" or, perhaps more precisely, "the inner state of a person who behaves in a morally acceptable manner." Kierkegaard's point is that such an inner state, far from being identical with faith, can be its opposite in the case where a person sees ethical behavior as something one can engage in autonomously. So to think of sin simply as the opposite of virtue is doubly misleading for Kierkegaard. It puts the emphasis on outer behavior rather than inner dispositions; even if we take virtue to be an inner disposition, it disguises the fact that a disposition to morally correct behavior can still be an expression of prideful autonomy from God. Hence sin must be contrasted with faith, not moral virtue.

A crucial aspect of Kierkegaard's definition of faith is the metaphor of transparency. What does it mean to rest transparently in God? It means, I think, to be totally open and honest with God and with oneself. To be transparent is to have nothing to hide. Of course, I cannot really hide anything from an omniscient God, so Kierkegaard's meaning here must be that I *willingly* reveal everything and anything to God. This requires self-understanding on my part. I must be willing to stand before God and open myself to his gaze. So long as I hide anything from myself, I cannot willingly reveal it to God.

If faith requires transparency, sin involves opacity. The individual who fails to be a self before God will lack clarity about herself.

We can see that Kierkegaard's psychology will be a depth psychology. It assumes that an individual will be unconscious of many aspects of her own personality. This depth psychology, however, differs significantly from Freudian psychology. For Kierkegaard, the unconscious is not simply a biological precipitate; it is something I form as I act and relate to others, and therefore I am at least partly responsible for it.

Anxiety and the Possibility of Sin

Strictly speaking, Kierkegaard says, sin is not something psychology or any other science can deal with.[1] We discover the true character of sin only when God reveals our sinfulness to us. Sin is a theological concept, not a psychological one. To this end Kierkegaard makes a distinction between the consciousness of sin and the consciousness of guilt. Human beings are capable of feeling guilty, even neurotically and inordinately so, but they are still convinced there is some way to overcome the problem and repair the damage through their own efforts. Sin is, however, a condition of alienation from God caused by our prideful autonomy. Attempting to overcome sin by our efforts is merely a way of compounding the problem, miring ourselves still deeper in the illusion that we can be ourselves without depending wholly on God.

Sin cannot be explained because it is rooted in freedom, and we cannot explain what causes a free choice. If an action had to occur, if we could point to its cause, then it would not have been a free action.[2] Kierkegaard refers to this quality of originality, which is part of any genuinely free action, as a *leap.*[3] A free action is a leap because it is discontinuous from the past. Nothing in the past guaranteed that the free action would occur. Something is genuinely different from what might have been, because of the choice.

Though every free choice is a leap, Kierkegaard tends to reserve this term for those choices that introduce a significant, qualitative change in a person's character—such as the leap from innocence to sin. The term is also used for the transition from sin to Christian faith, and we will discuss the "leap of faith" at some length later. However, it is important to see that the concept of the leap is a general category in Kierkegaard's thought, not a desperate invention to save Christianity, and that it has its natural home in the realm of human action.

Though sin lies outside the boundaries of psychology, it does border on psychology in several respects. Psychology can explore the antecedents of sin, the psychological conditions that make sin possible. Psychology can also explore the consequences of sin, the effects of sin on the human personality. I will explore sin in both contexts.

In Kierkegaard's thought, the antecedent of sin is *anxiety,* a term fraught with importance in the history of clinical psychology. Kierkegaard's understanding of anxiety is vastly different from that of either Freud or contemporary behavioral therapists. He sees it as the companion of freedom. It is not simply a result of repressed sexuality, as in the early Freud, or a signal of some threat to the personality, as the later Freud tends to assume. Nor is anxiety simply a conditioned response to some frightening stimulus, as early behaviorist psychologists thought. Anxiety is intimately related to sin and the destructive outcomes of sin in the personality, but it is not pathological. It is an integral element in our humanness.

Kierkegaard defines anxiety as a "sympathetic antipathy and an antipathetic sympathy."[4] In other words, anxiety is the experience of being both attracted to and repulsed by the same thing. Some contemporary psychologists have understood this and related anxiety to what they term "approach-avoidance conflicts." These psychologists have not, however, seen how profoundly this experience speaks of human freedom. In the human situation we find ourselves constantly pulled in opposite directions. A young man wants to get married, yet he does not want to get married. A young woman wants to go to college, yet she is afraid to go to college.

A person can act freely and responsibly without experiencing anxiety. We are free and responsible in instances when our desires are unambiguous also. However, the experience of anxiety gives us humans an awareness of our freedom and responsibility. It helps us see that life consists of choices. We might say that anxiety is *a revelatory emotion*. It reveals to us our spiritual character by signaling our freedom.

Anxiety and Original Sin

Anxiety, for Kierkegaard, is not the cause of sin, and it does not explain why human beings sin. However, it does explain why it is possible for human beings to sin. To understand this, we must focus on a special type of anxiety, which I shall call *fundamental anxiety*.

Kierkegaard believes that God created human beings as essentially good. How did sin enter the world? Kierkegaard attempts to answer this question through an analysis of original sin. How was it even possible for Adam and Eve to be tempted? God did not create them with overpowering lusts or evil desires. He did, however, endow them with freedom, and with freedom came fundamental anxiety.

We saw in the previous chapter that Kierkegaard sees persons as fundamentally dependent on God, yet free to ground themselves in what is less than God. To turn from God is to turn away from being our true selves. Fundamental anxiety is an awareness of the possibility of one's nothingness. It is an awareness that, though God has created me and endowed me with freedom, I can use this freedom to cut myself off from God and will my own destruction. Hence Kierkegaard describes anxiety as a fear that lacks a determinate object;[5] in anxiety I am afraid, but not afraid of this or that. I am afraid of nothing in particular, but "nothing" is not merely the lack of something; it is a condition I experience as my own possibility. Anxiety is not truly "objectless fear," as some have said, since this possibility is not truly nothing. The "object" in such a case is not a particular object; it cannot be identified with illness, job loss, or even physical death. It is the essentially ambiguous possibility that I may fail to be anything at all.

Terrifyingly, this possibility both repulses and attracts me. I want to will my own independence and autonomy, even if it means my destruction. So the answer to the question about the origin of Adam and Eve's temptation is that it lies in freedom itself. The temptation was to "lay hold of" one's freedom by declaring independence from God.[6] God cannot create free beings to relate freely to him without conceding to them this possibility.

Kierkegaard takes original sin very seriously. He employs the standard Danish theological term *Arvesynd*, which literally means "inherited sin." He does not doubt that sin entered the world with the very first humans, and he recognizes that sin is transmitted from generation to generation. While sexuality itself is certainly not sinful, human sexuality as it exists concretely is thoroughly permeated by sin.[7]

Understanding original sin is no easy matter, but Kierkegaard has some valuable hints as to how the subject should be approached. First, we must understand our sinfulness in a manner that does not let us off the hook by blaming it all on Adam and Eve.[8] Sin cannot be understood simply as an inherited physical ailment; it is a spiritual sickness. To avoid this simplification, Kierkegaard says, we must understand that the human race is a genuine unity. Without questioning the historicity of Adam, Kierkegaard insists that in some sense Adam is every person, and in some sense every person is Adam. Every person, including Adam, is "both himself and the race."[9] When Adam fell into sin, he in some way embodied and represented us all. When we fall into sin, we in some way recapitulate and repeat Adam's sin.

We have already seen that the question of why Adam and Eve sinned cannot be answered scientifically. Sin is the result of freedom. For the same reason the question "why does everyone sin?" is unanswerable. We cannot say why all human beings sin any more than we can say why Adam sinned. As Kierkegaard puts it, "Sin came into the world by a sin."[10] All we can say is that all humans do sin, and they thereby demonstrate the unity of the race.

We come closest to understanding sin by dealing with it existentially. Sin came into the world in the case of Adam and Eve and in the case of every individual as it came into our own person. Kierkegaard says, "How sin came into the world, each man understands solely by himself."[11]

Since we cannot explain scientifically why every human being sins, Kierkegaard tells each of us to reflect on our experience. Why have we sinned? To ask about sin from some objective point of view is to have misunderstood: "So when the single individual is stupid enough to inquire about sin as if it were something foreign to him, he only asks as a fool, for either he does not know at all what the question is about, and thus cannot come to know it, or he knows it and understands it, and also knows that no science can explain it to him."[12]

If we say that every person is Adam and in some way repeats Adam's fall into sin, does this commit us to Pelagianism, the doctrine that sin is only transmitted environmentally, and that human beings are therefore not born in sin? Not at all, according to Kierkegaard. Pelagianism does not recognize the overall effects of sin on the race. Sin does have a history, and this history will have consequences for our biological descendants.[13]

Kierkegaard resolves the apparent tension between the reality of the historical consequences of sin and the responsibility of individuals for their own sin by making a distinction between what he calls the qualitative and quantitative dimensions of sin. Adam's sin has thoroughly altered the character of human nature, even to the point of distorting our sexuality.[14] Human beings do not begin with a fresh slate. Besides the environmental influences, which even Pelagius recognized, people are born with a host of sinful inclinations. Kierkegaard calls such a state "sinfulness," and he distinguishes it from actual sin. Truly the cards are stacked against us. We are biological creatures, and our sinfulness has shaped our natural desires. Kierkegaard expresses this by saying that though sinfulness is not identical with our natural, sensuous urges such as sexuality, as a result of our sin our sensuousness, including sexuality, has become sinful.[15]

Though we inherit a sinful nature from Adam, our sinfulness is not itself sin. The sins of the human race, beginning with Adam, have produced changes in our sinfulness, but Kierkegaard describes these changes as quantitative. We have *more* sinful inclinations, but no matter how great our sinfulness, there is never a direct or automatic transition from sinfulness to actual sin. That transition is a qualitative one. Despite the quantitative changes that can be traced to Adam, we are still in Adam's position qualitatively. None of us can claim to have always done what we could and should; none of us can blame all our misdeeds on our environment and heredity. In willing to be our autonomous selves, distorted and shrunken as we are, we put ourselves in Adam's place. We too have a kind of innocence that we forfeit. By endorsing Adam's choice, we are saying in effect that we would have done the same thing if we had been in Adam's place.

Once original sin is accepted as a reality, the character of anxiety is transformed. It still is not inherently pathological. It retains its character as a signal or clue to our spirituality; it can be the emotion that spiritually awakens a person and starts him or her on the road to spiritual health. "Whoever has learned to be anxious in the right way has learned the ultimate."[16] A consistent theme in Kierkegaard is the way so-called negative emotions can have positive value if they are responded to in the right manner. Thus, if properly understood, anxiety can be excellent preparation for the gospel. "Therefore he who in relation to guilt is educated by anxiety will rest only in the Atonement."[17]

Nevertheless, in sinful human beings the positive value of anxiety is only a possibility. Anxiety is not only the psychological precondition for sin; it is the result of sin. Sinful humans remain anxious, and the character of their anxiety is transformed, just as their own character is transformed.[18] As they experience themselves as guilty, guilt itself becomes the source of anxiety. I fear and evade my guilt, yet cling to it. However painful guilt may be, it is mine, a proof of my control and independence. The hardest thing for people to do is to allow God to forgive them. The relief that freedom from guilt promises must be balanced by the acknowledgment of one's dependence on God.

For Kierkegaard, this means that while anxiety is not inherently pathological, it has taken on a pathological character in sinful creatures. The connections therapists have discovered between anxiety and pathology are genuine, and Kierkegaard knows that anxiety is far from healthy in experience.

Actual human beings are anxious about their sexual urges, their careers, their social status, their basic identity, what they will eat or drink tomorrow. The truly demonic person is even anxious about the idea that he might weaken and do something good! The healthy personality has learned in faith not to be anxious about any of these things. He has learned to "take no thought for tomorrow," because "your heavenly father knows that you need these things." To the degree that my identity is grounded in the God who created me, I cannot be anxious about finite, worldly matters.

Sin and Despair

The most characteristic manifestation of sin for Kierkegaard is not anxiety, but despair. Yet despair is more than a manifestation of sin; rightly understood, despair is sin and sin is despair.

Kierkegaard understands despair first and foremost not as a feeling, but as a state or condition. The condition of despair gives rise to the feeling we call despair when a person becomes aware of her true condition.

In ordinary speech we equate despair with loss of hope, and this is correct as far as it goes. A woman loses her job and then despairs. A man loses the woman he loves and then despairs. Each has lost hope. It appears in such a case that the object of despair is the job or the lover. The person thinks, "If I still had my job (or lover) I would not be in despair." But the despair is really over the self. The woman who despairs because she lost a job is really saying she cannot bear to be herself, her actual self. If she had that job, she thinks, things would be different. The man who despairs over the loss of a woman is in the same situation; he cannot accept himself as he is.

All despair, therefore, must be seen as despair of the self (p. 20). Despair is basically a failure to be my self, a failure to be a self at all. Being aware of this failure constitutes the feeling of despair. It is a feeling of one's own nothingness and worthlessness. However, it is very possible for someone to fail to be himself without recognizing this failure. Someone can be nothing without noticing his or her own nothingness. Thus, there can be unconscious despair, the condition of someone who is refusing to be a self but does not recognize this.

Once we recognize that despair can be unconscious, that it is a state in which we fail to be ourselves, and unite this insight with the Christian understanding that to be ourselves is to be continuously dependent on God, we can see that despair follows directly from sinfulness. In declaring independence from God, people are committing themselves to a life of despair. In accepting the Christian teaching that we are all indeed sinners, Kierkegaard is thus committed to accepting the claim that we are all in despair. He does not flinch from this conclusion:

> Just as a physician might say that there very likely is not one single living human being who is completely healthy, so anyone who really knows mankind might say that there is not one single living human being who does not despair a little, who does not secretly harbor an unrest, an inner strife, a disharmony, an anxiety about an unknown something or a something he does not even dare to try to know, an anxiety about some possibility in existence or an anxiety about himself. . . . In any case, no human being ever lived and no one lives outside of Christendom who has not despaired, and no one in Christendom if he is not a true Christian, and insofar as he is not wholly that, he still is to some extent in despair (p. 22).

Kierkegaard would say that those who find his view of human nature too gloomy have a superficial understanding of what it means to be a human being. No doubt there are millions of people who feel no despair, but for Kierkegaard that would only indicate how unconscious people are of their spiritual condition and how far they are from truly spiritual existence. "Not being in despair, not being conscious of despair, is precisely a form of despair" (p. 23). This is so because a lack of consciousness of despair can stem from a failure to understand what it is to be a self. In other words, I am not aware of my failure to be a self because I do not even know what it would be like to be a self.

The Christian psychologist should reject any superficial view of human nature that denies the reality of sin and despair. Instead, he or she must seek to understand human beings as they actually are, guided by the insight that they are dependent on God yet sinfully in rebellion against God, using the freedom that God has granted to them.

Notes

1. Søren Kierkegaard, The Concept of Anxiety, ed. and trans. Reidar Thomte (Princeton: Princeton University Press, 1980), 14.

2. See, for example, The Concept of Anxiety, 49, where it is said that sin cannot come into the world by necessity.

3. The "leap" is discussed frequently in The Concept of Anxiety in connection with the transition from innocence to sinfulness.

4. Kierkegaard, The Concept of Anxiety, 42.

5. Ibid., 43.

6. Ibid., 61.

7. Ibid., 67, 75.

8. Ibid., 35.

9. Ibid., 28.

10. Ibid., 32.

11. Ibid., 51.

12. Ibid., 50.

13. Ibid., 34–35.

14. Ibid., 49.

15. Ibid., 58.

16. Ibid., 155.

17. Ibid., 162.

18. Ibid., 54.

CHAPTER 5

Kierkegaard's Depth Psychology II: The Analysis of Despair

Kierkegaard analyzes despair from two different perspectives. First he looks at the objective condition of the despairer, disregarding the despairer's consciousness. We can call this a symptomatic analysis in that it focuses on the outcome of despair in the personality. Kierkegaard then analyzes despair from a more subjective viewpoint, focusing on the degree of consciousness of despair that is present in the despairer. Each type of analysis leads to different ways of categorizing the different kinds of despair. Each has value and importance in helping us understand the despair in ourselves and others.

The Symptomatic Analysis of Despair

We should bear in mind the ideal of personality that we examined in chapter 3 as we look at the concrete consequences of despair in the personality. There we looked at human persons as "relational syntheses." A human being is created by God as an unfinished synthesis of the eternal and the temporal, the infinite and the finite, soul and body. Our spirituality lies in our being active shapers, not just passive products, of this synthesis. The God who has created us as syntheses of these contrasting elements allows us to "relate ourselves to ourselves," which we can do successfully by consciously relating to God himself, or unsuccessfully by grounding our identity in what is less than God.

When a person breaks the God-relationship and falls into despair, the concrete result is that the synthesis becomes distorted. One of the elements present in a balanced tension in a healthy human personality remains underdeveloped and is dominated by the other. This one-sideness can take a variety of forms.

The nature of these distortions is shaped by the elements of the synthesis. The first section of *The Sickness unto Death* describes the self as composed of "the infinite and the finite, of the temporal and the eternal, of freedom and necessity" (p. 13). The descriptions of despair follow this definition in a formulaic—or as Kierkegaard himself says, "algebraic"—manner. The despair of infinitude consists in a lack of finitude, while the despair of finitude consists in a corresponding lack of infinitude. The despair of possibility lacks necessity, while the despair of necessity is said to lack possibility.

Interestingly, Kierkegaard does not delineate types of despair for temporality and eternity. Perhaps he has left that for readers to do on their own. More likely it is a clue that these different elements in the personality are not really distinct, but are merely different ways of describing one bipolar tension in the composition of the self. Infinitude, possibility, and eternity are three different ways of designating the expansive, future-oriented, ideal pole in the self, while finitude, necessity, and temporality are three ways of referring to the limited, contingent factor in the self. Each term has its characteristic connotations, and each may be said to reflect a slightly different aspect of its pole. Nevertheless, the despair of infinitude is strikingly similar to the despair of possibility, while the despair of necessity again is almost identical to the despair of finitude.

Having delineated these four forms, Kierkegaard has no need to go on with a description of the despair of eternity and the despair of temporality because essentially they have already been covered. In my discussion, therefore, I will delineate only two fundamental types: the infinite/possibility type of despair and the finite/necessity type. To simplify the discussion I shall sometimes refer to these simply as the despair of possibility and the despair of necessity, but I shall draw on descriptions taken from the discussion of infinitude and finitude as well.

A. The Despair of Infinitude/Possibility

Each type of despair is characterized by a lack of the contrasting element. Hence the despair of possibility is a result, not of too much possibility, but of too little necessity. It is not a matter of a person having dreams that are too grand or ideals that are too lofty, but of a failure to bring these dreams and ideals into relation with the grubby necessities of life.

This kind of despairer is described by Kierkegaard as "fantastic"—not in the sense of being wonderful, but in the more basic sense that one's life is primarily lived through fantasy. Imagination is essential to human existence; without imagination we could neither know, will, nor feel. Imagination lifts us above the realm of the actual to the possible. We orient our lives around what is not yet but could be, as well as the actual. It is possible, however, for a person to become intoxicated with the possible, to lose touch with the limits existence imposes on us. Such a person is in the grip of the despair of possibility.

Concrete examples come readily to mind. Kierkegaard says we can become fantastic with respect to feeling, knowledge, or will (p. 30). People who lack concreteness in their emotional life are comfortable with abstractions, but uneasy around other people. Think of the person who loves humanity but dislikes the shabby-looking person sitting at the other end of the pew in church. This sort of person claims to feel deeply about the poor, the homeless, and the hungry, and perhaps he does have powerful feelings; but these feelings never express themselves in concrete actions. Such a person possesses what we call sentimentality, but not genuine emotion.

With respect to knowledge, Kierkegaard thinks that in a healthy self, increasing knowledge goes hand in hand with increasing self-knowledge (p. 31). The "fantastic" knower is the person who somehow thinks that knowing a lot about astronomy, the Greek philosophers, or world history is sufficient to make him or her a genuine self. It is possible, however, to know an encyclopedia's worth of facts and never have an inkling of what life is all about. Such a person may know a lot about the great lovers of history, but have no understanding of love; may know about many courageous deeds, but have no sense of what courage is; may be able to recite stirring tales of devotion and loyalty, but be personally capable of the most mean-spirited and thoughtless betrayal.

The problem is not too much knowledge, but inhuman knowledge, knowledge without a human context of meaning. Even "useless" knowledge can be significant and human, if such knowing brings joy or if acquiring it entails self-discipline and personal development; but the mark of the inhuman knower is that the human significance of what is known is forgotten.

Kierkegaard describes a self that has become fantastic in willing as having been volatilized (p. 32). It is as if the self has become a vapor and lost any determinate shape or form. We all know people who are full of grand schemes and plans that never amount to anything, always turning over a "new leaf" and making new resolutions. There is nothing wrong with grand visions. Would that everyone could say with the late Martin Luther King, Jr., "I have a dream." The problem arises when people with dreams fail to carry out "the infinitely small part of the work that can be accomplished this very day, this very hour, this very moment" (p. 32).

Though I tread cautiously here, since I am not a psychologist and have no clinical experience to back up the suggestion, I wonder if Kierkegaard's concept of the despair of possibility or infinitude provides one useful way of thinking about some kinds of schizophrenia. Is not the schizophrenic a person who has no genuine identity, who has lost firm contact with reality? This perspective on schizophrenia at least has the merit of linking this problem to personality traits familiar to all of us. The schizophrenic, in this view, represents an extreme case of a kind of despair that many "normal" people exhibit.

Kierkegaard also gives hints that some other types of mental problems may be forms of the despair of possibility. A person in the grip of anxiety may let her imagination run wild with terrifying possibilities that may come to dominate her life. Such a person becomes a "victim of anxiety" (p. 37). Take for example a person with a phobia; the imagined possibilities that terrify her may have little relation to reality. Kierkegaard suggests that this victim of anxiety may consequently suffer from depression as well (p. 37).

Though we are tempted to say that this self in the grip of the despair of possibility has become unreal—and that is right in a way—Kierkegaard says it is more accurate to say that this self has lost necessity rather than reality (p. 36). Intoxicated by the possible, this personality cannot accept its status as a finite creature who can never be all it imagines. We might compare such a self to a person in a restaurant who has trouble ordering. I am one. I love to sit and think about the possibilities. To order is not only to risk regret that I have chosen wrongly, but to lose the wonderful feeling that I could have any of those things. However, a person who never orders gets nothing to eat, and a person who never makes a concrete choice never acquires a genuine identity.

It is important to see this distortion of the personality as a consequence of a break in the God-relationship. To acknowledge my dependence on God is to acknowledge that I am not God. I cannot be all things. I was born lacking certain abilities and skills. I will never run a four-minute mile or win a Nobel prize for physics. To live in possibility is to seek to hide this truth from myself; it is a way of evading my creatureliness and seeking to become as God. To live in faith, continually dependent on God, is to recognize that I was placed in a situation which is not of my own making (p. 36). I know I am not my own creator.

Thus true faith is an antidote to the despair of possibility. If Kierkegaard is correct, then Christian faith contains resources for dealing with some forms of psychological pathology, not merely the spiritual forms of pathology that are sometimes closely linked to the psychological.

B. The Despair of Finitude/Necessity

The despair of finitude/necessity is the opposite of the despair of infinitude/possibility. Kierkegaard in turn sees two versions of this: the despair of the social conformist and the despair of the fatalist.

Kierkegaard's descriptions of the social conformist contain some of his most poignant and familiar passages. This despairer is described as a person who forgets that God has created him as an individual. He has a unique divine name, but this person has forgotten it. "Surrounded by hordes of men, absorbed in all sorts of secular matters, more and more shrewd about the ways of the world—such a person forgets himself . . . finds it too hazardous to be himself and far easier and safer to be like the others, to become a copy, a number, a mass man" (pp. 33–34). These words seem so timely it is hard to believe they come from a book published in 1849!

Kierkegaard emphasizes how common such a personality is and how little the despair in such a case is likely to be noticed. A person in the grip of the despair of possibility is likely to seem a bit odd; the detachment from reality makes practical accomplishments difficult or impossible. However, the despair of necessity gives a person "an increasing capacity for getting along superbly in business and social life, indeed, for making a great success in the world" (p. 34).

One might think Kierkegaard's attack here is unfair. Are there not possibilities in the life of the social conformist? To understand Kierkegaard's answer to this criticism, we must see that there is a difference between *possibility* in the deepest sense and the realm of *probability*, which is what actually dominates the life of the conformist. Most of our lives are dominated by probabilities. This is not necessarily bad; there is a place for probability. It would be impossible, for example, for me to try to live without relying on my knowledge that I am more likely to do well on a test if I study or that I am more likely to be promoted if I work hard. The spiritual damage comes when probability becomes the whole of life.

All of us want certain things in life, and we calculate the odds of getting them and try to improve those odds. Suppose, however, that I am unlucky. I am the one who gets laid off or the one who is in the accident or the one who gets cancer. The wisdom of probability, which is worldly wisdom, can offer only more odds. Perhaps I can get a big settlement from the insurance company or find a physician to treat me who has an excellent cure ratio or somehow in some other way turn adversity into good fortune. Such advice can be sorry comfort for the person who has truly lost everything, and it ultimately reduces life to an enormous game of dice. Happiness is all a matter of luck, and it is easy to see why the survivors of a disaster often feel guilty. Why should they have been spared, while the others were unlucky?

The illusion of probability is the illusion that we are in control of our lives. The unfortunate person has had this illusion stripped away, but we may well wonder whether such a person might not in a sense be better off than the person who is "fortunate" enough to remain in the illusion. The person who despairs because of an *accident* was *essentially* in despair all along.

The human being whose life contains possibility in the deepest sense can look adversity in the face. This person truly trusts God, truly *believes* in him. His confidence is not in the odds, but in the heavenly Father who has promised never to leave him or forsake him. Such a person can hope even when, humanly speaking, the situation seems hopeless. His life is rooted in God, who is *the one for whom all things are possible* (p. 39). He can hope, like Abraham, that his descendants will be as numerous as the sand of the shore, even when he and his wife are past child-bearing age. She can hope, like Esther, that God will deliver her people through her, even though politically and pragmatically their destruction seems certain.

The fatalist represents the other type of the despair of necessity. Kierkegaard uses two wonderful metaphors to distinguish the role of possibility in the life of the healthy self and the fatalist. In the first, he compares possibility and necessity to vowels and consonants. The fatalist is like someone who must try to talk using only consonants: "If losing oneself in possibility may be compared with a child's utterance of vowel sounds, then lacking possibility would be the same as being dumb. The necessary is like pure consonants, but to express them there must be possibility. If this is lacking, if a human existence is brought to the point where it lacks possibility, then it is in despair" (p. 37).

Kierkegaard also uses the metaphor of breathing. "Personhood is a synthesis of possibility and necessity. Its continued existence is like breathing (respiration), which is an inhaling and exhaling. The self of the determinist cannot breathe, for it is impossible to breathe necessity exclusively" (p. 40). Just as physical breathing requires oxygen, so spiritual breathing requires spiritual oxygen, which is possibility.

Earlier I tentatively suggested that though the despair of possibility is present in many "normal" people, it could be seen most clearly in the loss of contact with reality that characterizes some schizophrenics. Similarly, though the despair of necessity is very pervasive in human life generally, I believe some cases of clinical depression may present the most vivid picture of this kind of despair.

Depression for many is clearly linked to a loss of hope, of any genuine, meaningful possibilities. If I am a depressed person, I see myself as trapped, with either no possibilities at all or only possibilities that are trivial and meaningless. If this suggestion is sound, then depression is a malady that sometimes has spiritual roots.

The remedy for the despair of possibility is faith—the faith to accept one's finitude and creatureliness. The remedy for the despair of necessity is faith also. Faith has therapeutic value in this case because God is the foundation of possibility. For God all things are possible, and it is he who makes hope possible in every situation. We see the presence of possibility in human life in prayer, and prayer lies at the very heart of what is distinctively human. "That God's will is the possible makes me able to pray; if there is nothing but necessity, man is essentially as inarticulate as the animals" (pp. 40–41).

Despair from the Viewpoint of Consciousness: Active and Passive Despair

While looking at the effects of despair on the personality, Kierkegaard also considers a more subjective perspective, the degree of a person's consciousness of despair. This level of awareness falls somewhere along a continuum from unconscious despair at one extreme to a despair that consciously, intensely defies God at the other. Whether either extreme is ever realized in life seems dubious. On the one hand, as we shall see when we discuss his view of the unconscious, Kierkegaard believes no person is completely without insight, at least at some points in life. Thus despair is perhaps never

THE ANALYSIS OF DESPAIR

totally unconscious, even if it expresses itself only occasionally as an anxiety or dark foreboding. On the other hand, Kierkegaard wonders whether despair is compatible with complete lucidity about one's condition. Such a lucid despair would be demonic, and Kierkegaard says that Satan himself is the paradigm for conscious despair (p. 42). Human beings may not be capable of such defiance. Some self-deception and obscuring of the truth may be necessary to keep the game going.

Though the consciousness of despair ranges on a continuum, Kierkegaard still finds it useful to delineate despair in terms of two fundamental types. Despair, he says, can take an essentially active or essentially passive form. One can be in despair by *failing to be* oneself, but also by *being* oneself. This is initially confusing, but important in understanding the essentially Christian character of Kierkegaard's view.

If the self were autonomous or self-creating, says Kierkegaard, then there would be only one type of despair, namely, failing to be oneself. Such a view captures nicely what is often thought of as the existentialist conception of the self. If I create myself, then I am my own god. I cannot choose wrongly; the only sin is failing to choose.

However, the self is not autonomous in this way from Kierkegaard's perspective. I become a self by "relating myself to myself," but I do that only by "relating myself to another." The self is a gift from God. It is a gift that includes possibilities, so I must choose to affirm the self God has created me to be. Nevertheless, the self is chosen, not created. This means that despair can take two forms. I can passively fail to be the self God intends, or I can actively refuse to be the self God intends, by misusing the freedom granted me and choosing to be some other self.

Actually the contrast drawn here is only relatively valid. Kierkegaard says there is always an element of activity in passive despair, since failing to be the self God intends is an act of disobedience. Also, there is an element of passivity, of weakness, even in the most active despair, since in the end the self the despairer wills to be is a self that he *is not* and never can be (p. 20).

Kierkegaard also calls these two forms of despair "masculine" and "feminine." Many readers have accused him of sexism for this differentiation, and the charge may have some justification. However, if we recognize that Kierkegaard is here talking of sexuality as it exists in a sinful race, and that our society—like his—is dominated by sexual stereotypes that have real cultural power, his terminology is very illuminating. Women are commonly socialized to be more passive than men, and men are usually socialized to be more aggressive than women. (Socialization definitely plays a major role, but I shall not try to say whether there are also biological components.)

There are naturally exceptions to this generalization (as Kierkegaard acknowledges in a note on page 49), but to the extent that it is true, it is reasonable to see gender as making a difference in the forms of despair, shaping the specific character of pathology. Mary Stewart Van Leeuwen has argued that at least in our culture, the sinfulness of women is likely to take the form of passively submitting to injustice and exploitation, while the sinfulness of men is more likely to take the form of active domination.[1] It is important to note that Kierkegaard does not make a similar differentiation between men and women with respect to health, at least ideally; both men and women become their true selves by giving themselves to God in devotion (p. 50n).

The Continuum of Despair

On the continuum of degrees of consciousness of despair, Kierkegaard differentiates at least four major types of despair. First, he distinguishes conscious from unconscious despair, though as we have noted, this is a relative distinction since despair is probably never totally conscious or totally unconscious. Within the category of conscious despair, the despair of weakness, failing to be yourself, is distinguished from the despair of defiance, boldly willing to be yourself. Within the category of weakness, despair over the earthly is distinguished from despair over the eternal. All these positions can be seen on the line on the following page.

As one moves to the right on this line, the type of despair becomes increasingly unusual, according to Kierkegaard. Unconscious despair, or the despair that is ignorant of being despair, is by far the most common type. Such a despair, in comparison with more active, defiant forms, almost possesses a kind of innocence. Here the problem with the person is simply that she does not understand that she was created to be spirit.

The Continuum of Despair

Unconscious Despair	Conscious Despair
	Despair of Weakness Despair of Defiance
	Despair over the Earthly Despair over the Eternal

◀— Less consciousness   More consciousness —▶

This does not mean, of course, that the person cannot live an active and even satisfying life when judged by unspiritual standards of satisfaction. A person who achieves amazing things or experiences delightful pleasures or who knows all she could know about science nevertheless must be judged to have missed out on understanding what life is meant to be if she does not understand herself as standing before God:

> Every human existence that is not conscious of itself as spirit or conscious of itself before God as spirit, every human existence that does not rest transparently in God but vaguely rests in and merges in some abstract universality (state, nation, etc.) or, in the dark about his self, regards his capacities merely as powers to produce without becoming deeply aware of their source, regards his self, if it is to have intrinsic meaning, as an indefinable something—every such existence, whatever it achieves, be it most amazing, whatever it explains, be it the whole of existence, however intensively it enjoys life esthetically—every such existence is nevertheless despair (p. 46).

Though unconscious despair seems almost innocent in comparison with defiant despair, this does not mean that a person in this form of despair is nearer to salvation. To the contrary, a consciousness of despair, though it intensifies despair as long as she remains in despair, can wrench a person out of despair altogether. Remaining ignorant of one's despair can be a way of imprisoning the self in its deplorable condition.

The next stage up on the continuum is a form of the despair of weakness. Here the person consciously despairs, but lacks a true conception of despair nonetheless. This is despair over the earthly, as when a person is in despair because he lost his job or failed to get a raise or lost his girlfriend to someone else. Such a person does not wish to be himself any more; he may even wish to be someone else. If only things had gone differently, he would have been happy, but now he cannot stand himself.

In less severe cases of this type, the person despairs over some particular, earthly thing. A person with a little bit of reflective power may reach a deeper level of despair, despairing not just over this or that, but over the whole of earthly goods. Such a person realizes, however dimly, that he would not have been happy even if he had gotten the new job and could afford the BMW. Such a person is on the verge of understanding what human life is all about; he has arrived at the boundary of understanding his own spirituality.

All too often such a spiritual insight is covered over again by the dimness of probability and worldly wisdom, which "rescues" the person from despair by essentially draining from him any trace of individuality. He is once more taught to be like the others, a faceless, anonymous conformist who does not despair because he has no dreams or hopes except those that fit into the great probability calculus of life.

The person who does not fall into this trap may move into the next phase, despair over the eternal. Kierkegaard describes the difference between this despair and the previous kind as follows: "If the preceding despair was *despair in weakness*, then this is *despair over his weakness* " (p. 61). If I have discovered my spiritual nature through despair of the earthly, it is possible to sink still deeper by despairing that I am so weak as to be trapped by things that I know have only ephemeral value.

This kind of despair, which is indeed rare, expresses itself in a sort of hidden self that Kierkegaard calls *Indeslut-tethed*, a word which is very difficult to translate. Literally "shut-up-ness," it is often translated "enclosing reserve." Such a person may be outwardly well-adjusted and sociable, but the outwardness is only a "false door" that the true self hides behind. He has a craving for solitude, and there is a genuine danger of suicide. If the person can somehow open himself up to someone, share his dreadful secret with a confidante, then his enclosing reserve will probably be "moderated" (p. 66). This moderation is healthy unless the person begins to despise himself for his weakness in opening up to another person, in which case suicide looms again as a real possibility.

The final and most intense form of despair is the most active, the despair of defiance. Here the person comes to understand that despair is not something that happens to him, but something he has chosen. We shall see in chapter 7 that such despair is in one sense close to salvation, but as long as the person continues in despair it is in another sense very far from true selfhood.

Kierkegaard calls this form of despair "stoicism," though he recognizes that the name does not quite fit what he has in mind (p. 68). I believe that if he were writing today, Kierkegaard would call this form of despair "existentialism," for it fits some of the formulations of twentieth-century existentialism precisely. (This is wonderful irony, given the popular view of Kierkegaard as the father of existentialism.) In the despair of defiance a person is unwilling to accept the self he has been given, but wants to create himself from scratch. Relying on the freedom given him by God, he wants to become his own god. He wants to see himself, in Nietzschean or Sartrean fashion, as the author of values, the creator of good and evil. This personality, according to Kierkegaard, can never really become a self, but can only generate an appearance of a unified spiritual reality:

> If the self in despair is an *acting self*, it constantly relates itself to itself only by way of experiments, no matter what it undertakes, . . . It recognizes no power over itself; therefore it basically lacks earnestness and can conjure forth only an appearance of earnestness, even when it gives its utmost attention to its experiments. . . . Like Prometheus stealing fire from the gods, this is stealing from God the thought—which is

earnestness—that God pays attention to one; instead the self in despair is satisfied with paying attention to itself (pp. 68–69).

The problem with such a quest for autonomy is that serious values and obligations must come to me from a transcendent source. They must be recognized and cannot be created. If I know that the only reason something has value is that I have arbitrarily decided to bestow value upon it, I simultaneously know that I could withdraw the value at any moment. Thus what I value is in reality valueless, and it is only self-deception that enables me to forget this. Kierkegaard says this "absolute ruler is a king without a country, actually ruling over nothing" (p. 69). This is so because his sovereignty is subject to the condition that a rebellion is at any moment legitimate (p. 69).

Why hold onto despair in such a case? In one sense there is no good reason; that is why self-deception (which we will consider in the next chapter) is necessary for despair. Nevertheless, we can see a certain logic to despair, which becomes increasingly clear in its higher forms. Even if a person is in despair, it is still *his* despair. Despair is thus in the end a kind of pride, a form of rebellion against God. People prefer despair and autonomy, even pseudo-autonomy, to health and trust in God.

Notes

1. See Mary Stewart Van Leeuwen, "Christian Maturity in Light of Feminist Theory," *Journal of Psychology and Theology* 16, no. 2 (1988): 168–82.

CHAPTER 6

Kierkegaard's Depth Psychology III: Sin, Self-Deception, and the Unconscious

In looking at Kierkegaard's analyses of anxiety and despair it becomes evident how important the concept of the unconscious is to his psychological thought. The notion of the self's opacity to itself lies at the heart of Kierkegaard's understanding of sin. Both despair and anxiety presuppose a self that is not completely lucid about its doings; in fact, unconscious anxiety and despair are by far the most common forms. It is worthwhile, therefore, to focus more attention on this crucial concept. What is the unconscious for Kierkegaard? How does it develop? How does it function? Can it be healed?

The Unconscious as Rooted in Relations with Others

We saw in chapter 4 how Kierkegaard's view of the unconscious is different from Freud's. Actually there is a tension within Freud's own view. In his early work Freud tends to see the unconscious as a mass of instinctual drives, biologically grounded forces that shape the personality. Later on, Freud recognizes that the phenomenon he called "repression" implies that some aspects of the unconscious are not simply biological, but are developed as the person deals with unresolved conflicts. I can only repress what I am in some sense already aware of.

Several schools of Freud's followers have picked up on

this later perspective of the unconscious as something that evolves. The curiously named "object-relations" school, for example, rooted in the work of English psychoanalyst W. D. Fairbairn and popularized by Harry Guntrip, completely rejects Freud's biological theory of instincts as the key to understanding the unconscious. According to this theory, the unconscious develops as the person's psychological identity develops. The key to understanding this process of development is to understand the individual's relationship with significant others, called "objects" in psychoanalytic jargon (hence the name of the school).

The primary developmental task, in this view, is the passage from infantile dependence to a kind of mature dependence compatible with having an identity of one's own. My identity is initially united with the primary care-giver, which is traditionally the mother in most societies. Since the mother cannot possibly satisfy all my desires, I form images of both a "good" and "bad" mother and incorporate these into my sense of self. The tension between the two images results in the child's dissociating them, or splitting them apart.[1] The "bad" self is somehow not really me.

Though this split develops in all of us to some degree, it is not too severe in people who have fairly adequate early parenting. However, a person who lacks the kind of love that provides what Guntrip calls "a basic security-giving relationship" will develop a defective form of what Freud called the superego, but which Guntrip prefers to call "the internal saboteur."[2]

We saw in chapter 3 that Kierkegaard, like the object-relations theorists, views the self as a thoroughly relational entity. Kierkegaard recognizes the role of early care-givers and significant others in the development of what we have termed "the pre-self." Such a grounding of the self in other finite selves is necessary and not pathological, although Kierkegaard is only too aware from his own childhood that this process can be distorted and the pre-self deformed through bad relations with others. It is only God who can provide the basis for a secure identity for the self. When the emerging self represses its awareness of God and tries to ground its identity in a God-substitute, the result is a divided self that is at least partially opaque to itself. This process of forming the unconscious we will explore in some depth.

There is a sense in which, for Kierkegaard, the unconscious is always present and does not have to be developed. In understanding the self as an achievement, something I must become, Kierkegaard has already distinguished his view from the sort of conception of the self associated with the French philosopher René Descartes. Descartes saw the self as a unified ego, a consciousness that was necessarily transparent to itself. What Descartes sees as the essence of the self, Kierkegaard views as the goal. Before selfhood proper begins, the pre-self is a complicated mixture of sometimes conflicting desires and tendencies. This is made possible by what we might term the self's "natural dissociation." That is, I am not clearly aware of every aspect of myself. The self contains within itself "obscure powers," to use a telling phrase from *Either-Or*, volume 2.[3]

We must distinguish, however, between what could be termed "the unnoticed unconscious" and what Freudians call "the dynamic unconscious." The dynamic unconscious is the aspect of the self that I have in some sense chosen to overlook or to obscure; it is not merely undiscovered. This dynamic unconscious is the real object of Kierkegaard's interest.

To understand the dynamic unconscious we must focus on the role played by a person's choices. Something like a dynamic unconscious is already present in my pre-self as conflicts in my identity develop through bad relations with others. However, it will be recalled that the decisive relation for the development of the self in the proper sense is God. Hence the decisive aspect of the unconscious develops as a result of my interaction with God. In attempting to hide my awareness of God from myself, I necessarily deceive myself, as I try to disown the wishes, desires, and choices that I know at bottom to be mine.

Kierkegaard's Understanding of Self-Deception: "Defenses"

Self-deception appears paradoxical, and some have alleged that it is literally impossible. To deceive myself I must know the truth and intentionally obscure the truth. But how can I convince myself that what I know to be true is not true? Such a project seems as difficult as trying not to think of a pink elephant: the harder one tries to do it, the more difficult the task becomes.

Kierkegaard's answer to this problem rests on the fact that human beings are temporal creatures and that the process of self-deception is therefore a temporal process. The problem is treated in *The Sickness unto Death* in at least a couple of passages, most notably in the course of analyzing the Socratic principle that sin is ignorance.

Kierkegaard agrees that from a Christian perspective this view in a sense is correct. Sin is a kind of ignorance or stupidity (p. 88). What the Socratic view does not recognize is that it is a willed ignorance, for which the individual is culpable. Obviously, however, to say that the ignorance is willed is to say that it involves self-deception, for in order to will to be ignorant of something I must in some way be aware of the knowledge that I will to suppress.

Ultimately, then, Kierkegaard wishes to trace evil back to the will. But he recognizes that it is rare if not impossible for the person simply to will what he knows to be evil. The normal process is for the will to corrupt one's knowledge; sin goes hand in hand with self-deception.

This process of corruption is a temporal one. When the will does not want to do what a person knows to be right, the usual response is not for the person to consciously do what he knows to be wrong, but simply to delay doing anything. "Willing allows some time to elapse, an interim called 'We shall look at it tomorrow'" (p. 94). This period of time allows the person to carry out any number of strategies to subvert his understanding. "The lower nature's power lies in stretching things out" (p. 94). Eventually, "little by little" (p. 56), Kierkegaard says, the understanding is changed so that knowing and willing can "understand each other," can "agree completely" (p. 94).

What are some of these strategies? One is simply to *delay*, to wait for the knowledge to decay. Since we have seen that human beings are not Cartesian selves, and since they are temporal creatures, delay may result in some dissociation "naturally." As Kierkegaard puts it, the knowledge simply "dims" or "becomes obscure." The fact that this is a natural process does not absolve the person of responsibility, for it is the willed delay that makes this dimming possible, and the person is guilty for the delay since it is motivated by the hope that just this dimming will occur. At particular moments the knowledge may come to consciousness, but over time these moments come more and more infrequently, and the consciousness involved becomes more and more dim.

A second strategy is *distraction*. In this the person does not merely wait for nature to take its course, but actively intervenes. "He may try to keep himself in the dark about his state through diversions and in other ways, for example, through work and business as diversionary means, yet in such a way that he does not entirely realize why he is doing it, that it is to keep himself in the dark" (p. 48).

Here Kierkegaard is helping us see that it *is* possible to intentionally avoid thinking of a pink elephant. Obviously we must think of a pink elephant at some time to have this intention, but the intention is nevertheless one that can be successfully carried out over time. Eventually we can put ourselves into a state in which we are not thinking of a pink elephant. The trick is diversion. We must focus on something else. If the something else is engrossing enough for us to lose ourselves in it, we will eventually forget the elephant.

In the same way, if we plunge into various activities— useful work, committees, sports, games, or even religious works—we may eventually find that the disturbing insights into who we are no longer haunt our consciousness. A person may even, Anti-Climacus says, do this with a certain shrewdness or insight into what is going on. That is, he may recognize in general terms that this process of diverting himself is a way of "sinking his soul in darkness" (p. 48). This is psychologically possible as long as the person does not clearly focus on the specific insights he wishes to avoid.

Such strategies could usefully be termed "defenses," to use Freudian language, since they are crucial not only in obscuring our self-knowledge originally, but also in keeping the troubling knowledge at bay. Kierkegaard does not systematically catalog the various defenses available to human beings, but he does give interesting and insightful analyses of several such strategies.

One of the most common and dangerous of these defenses might be termed "intellectualizing." The self-knowledge in question is existential, knowledge about how life should be lived. It is tempting for the person to substitute for such knowledge a kind of intellectual awareness. I convince myself that I am ethical because I know a lot about ethical theory. I convince myself that I am a Christian because I know a lot of theology. It is this kind of defense that Kierkegaard thinks the educated intellectual, "the professor," is particularly prone to—and he treats it with unwithering scorn.

Even Socrates recognized a difference between "understanding and understanding." Yet he failed to see that the intellectual understanding which in the genuine sense is no understanding at all is not merely ignorance. There is a difference between "not *being able* to understand and not *willing* to understand" (p. 95). Intellectual understanding can be a defense against genuine understanding.

Self-Deception and Sin

The paradox of self-deception and the difficulty of understanding it underlie one of the central problems of *The Sickness unto Death*, namely, the paradoxical attitude of Kierkegaard toward unconscious despair and toward paganism, the "despairing unconsciousness of God." On the one hand, Kierkegaard clearly wants to say that there can be unconscious despair. "Not being in despair, not being conscious of being in despair, is precisely a form of despair" (p. 23). On the other hand, unconscious despair does not quite seem to be despair in a full-blooded sense; such despair one is tempted, humanly speaking, to describe as a kind of innocence. "It is almost a dialectical issue whether it is justifiable to call such a state despair" (p. 42).

This ambivalence about unconscious despair is even more pronounced with respect to unconscious sin—as well it might be, since sin for Kierkegaard is an intensified form of conscious despair. Sin is a spiritual disorder, and a spiritless being would seem to be incapable of sin. Kierkegaard seems to view paganism as a kind of innocence: "The sin of paganism was essentially despairing ignorance of God, . . . Therefore, from another point of view, it is true that in the strictest sense the pagan did not sin, for he did not sin before God, and all sin is before God" (p. 81). Yet in the final analysis Kierkegaard is loathe to give the pagan a blanket dispensation and recognizes the strangeness of a view that absolves paganism of sin. "Christianity regards everything as under sin; we have tried to depict the Christian point of view as rigorously as possible— and then this strange outcome emerges, this strange conclusion that sin is not to be found at all in paganism but only in Judaism and Christendom, and there again very seldom" (p. 101).

So Kierkegaard retreats from the general absolution of the pagan and insists that the lack of consciousness which forms the basis of the pagan's "innocence" is itself culpable and must be seen, therefore, as grounded in self-deception. "Is it [being in a state of spiritlessness] something that happens to a person? No, it is his own fault. No one is born devoid of spirit, and no matter how many go to their death with this spirit-lessness as the one and only outcome of their lives, it is not the fault of life" (p. 102).

The problem is, this suggests that the ignorance cannot have been complete. One must have—or at least one must have had—spirit in order to have become spiritless. To be spiritless is to lack a consciousness of God. Kierkegaard's view here seems to lead to the conclusion that there is in every human being an original knowledge of God, a knowledge which becomes obscured and repressed over time but which is nonetheless enough to make the person responsible.

Is There a Natural Awareness of God In All Humans?

The view that there is something like a universal, natural knowledge of God is puzzling and difficult to accept, but it seems implicit at many points in Kierkegaard's writings and explicit at a few points. In the *Journals and Papers*, in a draft version of *Philosophical Fragments*, he says that there has never been a genuine atheist, only people who did not wish to "let what they knew, that God existed, get power over their minds."[4] In both *Postscript* and *Fragments,* the hostility to the idea of proving God's existence seems to be linked to the idea that such proofs are unnecessary because God is in some sense already present to human beings.[5]

We may reasonably ask about such a universal knowledge of God, "In what does it consist?" On the surface many people do not seem to have a conscious awareness of God. This observation is quite compatible with Kierkegaard's view, of course, since it is not his thesis that everyone is actually aware of God. The whole point of much of *The Sickness unto Death* is that this knowledge has become repressed and that understanding this repression is the key to understanding the unconscious in humans. Still, in order to repress this knowledge, humans must once have had it, and we may reasonably ask whether such a view is in accord with what we know about human psychological development.

To make sense of Kierkegaard's position, I think we must distinguish between a conscious awareness of God and a conscious awareness of God *as* God. It is implausible to claim that the latter kind of knowledge is universally present in human beings, even originally or as a kind of potential knowledge. It is not, however, absurd to maintain that human beings in fact have an awareness of God, even though they do not always understand that it is God whom they are aware of. Kierkegaard explicitly claims that it is *conscience* which constitutes the relationship to God (p. 124). This is consistent with the general Kierkegaardian view that the religious life, while never reducible to the ethical life, always arises out of a confrontation with ethical ideals. (We will examine Kierkegaard's view of the relation between the ethical life and the religious life in the next chapter.)

Not every child has a clear, explicit understanding of the nature of God. However, according to Kierkegaard, every child does encounter ideals that are experienced as absolute in character and, in experiencing these ideals, gains some sense of the "infinity" of the self. (A degree of cultural relativity in the content of the ideals does not matter, since it is their absolute form which is determinative.) In encountering such ideals I gain a sense of my self as more than a product of accidental circumstances. Rather, I am called to exercise responsible choice and become the ideal self I see it as my task to become. Whether the child understands this or not, this is an encounter with the ontological "other" that is the "power" that constitutes the self.

Conscience and the Self

The thesis that conscience is decisive in the development of the self is not unique to Kierkegaard. In a way this is Freud's view as well, since for Freud the resolution of the Oedipus conflict and the development of the superego are also decisive in becoming an adult.

The differences with Freud are more significant than the similarities, however. For Freud, the superego is simply the internalized parent; there is no question of its being in any sense the voice of God. It does not represent absolute truth but cultural relativity. For Kierkegaard, conscience, while certainly reflecting cultural norms, also reflects the emergence of a sense of one's own freedom and responsibility through an encounter with ideals that have absolute validity.

This difference leads me to believe that the Freudian superego and the Kierkegaardian conscience are not identical. I think this becomes evident in looking at the crucial time period when each is formed. For the superego the crucial age is clearly around three. However, this cannot be the crucial age for the development of conscience in the significant sense for Kierkegaard. Once conscience is in place, a person's capacity to despair and to sin is in place as well, but it is well known that Kierkegaard did not think very young children were capable of sin in any genuine sense. In *The Sickness unto Death* Kierkegaard says plainly that children are not capable of despair, but only bad temper (p. 49n). This doesn't mean that children do not have feelings of depression; it means rather that they are not capable of throwing away the self they were meant to be, because in the most profound sense they have not yet acquired enough self to be capable of such a choice.

I think, therefore, that we must look to late childhood or even adolescence as the crucial period for the emergence of conscience in the Kierkegaardian sense. (The exact age surely differs from child to child.) In adolescence the person discovers that she must choose and affirm—or reject—what has been handed down to her by culture. This call to responsible choice is at the same time a discovery that choices matter—that the person is called to choose responsibly. In Kierkegaard's language it is the discovery that she is spirit, and Kierkegaard interprets this encounter as God's call to the individual to become what God has created her to be.

Another significant difference between Freudian and Kierkegaardian views now comes into view, and that concerns the relation between conscience, pathology, and the unconscious. For Freud, the overactive superego is a source of pathology. It is the sadistic, internal saboteur that must be tamed and moderated for the sake of individual psychological health, even if we must retain it in some form for the sake of civilized society. Kierkegaard is hardly ignorant of the torments of the overly active conscience, given his own upbringing, but he is far from seeing this as the most significant source of human sickness.

Like Freud, Kierkegaard favors an approach to the child's development that avoids excessive guilt. The imposition of strict Christian concepts on the child is even characterized as "a rape, be it ever so well meant."[6] Children who are victims of such a rape have a struggle to endure as they attempt to come to terms with the love and forgiveness of God.

Despite this apparent agreement with Freud and neo-Freudians, who see the major problem of human life to be guilt feelings caused by an overactive superego, Kierkegaard would by no means be enthusiastic about banishing guilt from contemporary life. Our most pressing problem is not that we have excessive guilt feelings, but that we avoid coming to terms with the fact that we are really guilty.

The development of the pathological unconscious must be seen in connection with just this point. The motivation for the development of the unconscious is our sensuousness, our failure to rise above the categories of what feels pleasant and unpleasant, because the experience of guilt is decidedly unpleasant. Most human beings do not have "the courage to venture out and to endure being spirit" (p. 43).

So when the call of conscience comes, humans have a reason to ignore it. And once they have ignored it, they have a double reason for ignoring it, because to face conscience is to encounter not only the unpleasantness of responsible decision making, but also the greater unpleasantness of facing their decision to shirk responsibility. Thus the dynamic unconscious emerges, the long process of deceiving oneself about oneself, employing the strategies we have discussed as well as a host of others.

We have now given at least a rough account of what might be termed the doctrines of creation and sin in Kierkegaard's psychology. In chapter 3 we analyzed Kierkegaard's conception of human beings as God created them: spiritual beings who live in conscious dependence on God and in communion with each other. In chapters 4 through 6 we looked at the ways sin, a spiritual malady, has distorted our spirituality. We now need to consider the ways we can be healed.

Before turning our attention to the subject of healing, however, it will be helpful to take another look at the themes we have traversed already, by looking at Kierkegaard's picture of human psychological development. Here we have what we might call a longitudinal description of themes we have looked at in isolation. After a study of Kierkegaard's development perspective, we will return to the subject of faith as the overcoming of sin.

Notes

1. See chapter 3 of Harry Guntrip, *Psychoanalytic Theory, Therapy and the Self* (New York: Basic Books, 1971).

2. Ibid., 191.

3. Søren Kierkegaard, *Either/Or*, vol. 2, ed. and trans. Howard V. Hong and Edna H. Hong (Princeton: Princeton University Press, 1987), 164.

4. *Søren Kierkegaard's Journals and Papers*, vol. 3, ed. and trans. Howard V. Hong and Edna H. Hong (Bloomington: Indiana University Press, 1978), entry 3606.

5. For a typical passage see Kierkegaard's *Concluding Unscientific Postscript*, trans. David Swenson and Walter Lowrie (Princeton: Princeton University Press, 1968), 485.

6. Ibid., 524.

CHAPTER 7

Kierkegaard as Developmental Psychologist

We have looked in some detail at the ways a person fails to become a self. For Kierkegaard, the failure to live before God in trustful dependence on him leads to a disintegration of selfhood, a failure to become the person God intended. The result is a disunified self, opaque to itself, caught in despair and pathological anxiety.

It is appropriate now to look at the process of healing. To understand how a person can achieve the transparency before God that constitutes health, we need to know something about human development. In this chapter we will look at what might be termed Kierkegaard's developmental psychology, and this will lay a foundation for a discussion in the next chapter of the therapeutic insights Kierkegaard has to offer.

"The Stages on Life's Way"

Kierkegaard's developmental scheme is summarized in his well-known theory of "the stages on life's way." In this theory Kierkegaard defines three broad stages of human development: the aesthetic, the ethical, and the religious. Each of these stages has substages and variant forms.

Kierkegaard also calls these stages the three "spheres of existence." That the stages are also spheres is significant. In so designating them, Kierkegaard is underlining his conviction that humans are spiritual beings. As spiritual beings, their development is not a natural process in the same way that the acquisition of facial hair or wisdom teeth is. Rather, the development of selfhood requires the free participation of the person.

This means that although Kierkegaard considers it normal for healthy people to pass through those stages in a particular order and at roughly the same time in life, it is by no means inevitable or even common for this to occur. A person can become "fixated" at a particular stage and even choose to remain at this stage. When the stages are viewed in this way, as the object of fundamental life choices, they are properly described as spheres of existence, fundamentally different ways of living, which confront each other as rivals.

As we shall see, the theory of the stages is in one sense an idealized theory. It outlines an ideal process of development of an individual toward health, a process that will rarely occur in life. But the theory also takes into account the sinfulness of human life we have explored in the previous three chapters. It sketches what I would call "a realistic ideal"—an ideal process of human development given the reality of sin.

Kierkegaard's method of presenting the stages differs from mine. I shall explain the stages in a theoretical fashion. Kierkegaard does this also in places, but fundamentally he explains the three stages by confronting the reader with examples. This is, in fact, the key to understanding Kierkegaard's use of pseudonyms. He hoped that an understanding of the stages on life's way would lead to personal growth in at least some of his readers. Because of his stress on freedom, Kierkegaard knew there was no way he could guarantee this growth, no techniques by which to justify promising his readers that through his books they would achieve better mental health in thirty days. Nevertheless, he thought that growth would be more likely to occur if the reader could somehow be existentially engaged.

Rather than simply handing the reader a theory, which could easily be treated as a purely intellectual exercise (here we recall the danger of the defense of intellectualizing), Kierkegaard attempted to present literary embodiments of the stages on life's way. He hoped his readers' encounter with these literary personae—aesthetes, ethical persons, and religious persons—would be like looking in a mirror. He hoped they would experience a shock of self-recognition that would startle them into moving on to the next stage.

Thus when we turn to what Kierkegaard calls his "aesthetic authorship," we find that the books are not actually attributed to Kierkegaard. Instead they carry pseudonyms like Victor Eremita, Johannes de Silentio, and Constantine Constantius. These pseudonyms are not merely pen names, and they are certainly not an attempt to disguise the real author of the books. Rather, they are fictional *personae*, like characters in a novel, who have their own viewpoints on life. This makes reading Kierkegaard's pseudonymous works difficult. We must come to know the pseudonym and his perspective before we can hope to recognize what Kierkegaard himself is trying to show us.

For these reasons new readers of Kierkegaard are wise to begin with his nonpseudonymous, religious works such as *Works of Love*, because they give a relatively straightforward perspective on his thinking. Another good starting point is the works by Anti-Climacus, *The Sickness unto Death* and *Practice in Christianity*, which I have drawn heavily upon in these chapters. The Anti-Climacus pseudonym differs radically from the others in that it is a "Christian" pseudonym. Kierkegaard invented this name, not because he does not agree with the views represented, but because he thought he was personally too far from having realized the Christian ideals in his own life. The pseudonym allowed him to present Christianity in an ideal manner while at the same time preaching to himself, as it were.

In explaining Kierkegaard's developmental theory, I will make no attempt to emulate the skillful literary form he uses. I will lay out the theory in a fairly straightforward style, although I will try to describe some of the more memorable figures from his pseudonymous writings.

A. The Aesthetic Life: Living for the Moment

The aesthetic life is dominated by what others such as Freudians call impulse, desire, or instinctive drive. Kierkegaard calls this stage 'aesthetic' because the word is derived from the Greek *aisthesia*, meaning "sensation." He describes the aesthetic life in a variety of ways: the aesthete lives for the moment, lives for pleasure, lives to satisfy immediate desires.

It might be helpful to begin by comparing the aesthete to what philosophers call "the hedonist." Hedonism is the belief that pleasure is the sole intrinsic human good, and the hedonist therefore seeks a life as full of pleasure and as free from pain as possible. Kierkegaard's aesthete obviously resembles a hedonist, and I would even say that the hedonist is a common type of aesthete. Nevertheless, there are some subtle but significant differences.

In putting the emphasis on pleasure, hedonism obscures the fact that what a person wants is often not so much a particular outcome as *to have his own way*. As one of Kierkegaard's aesthetic pseudonyms put it, "If I had in my service a submissive jinni who, when I asked for a glass of water, would bring me the world's most expensive wines, deliciously blended, in a goblet, I would dismiss him until he learned that the enjoyment consists not in what I enjoy but in getting my own way."[1] Anyone who has watched children play can verify that very often they want a toy only because someone else wants it; the child may want the toy to show that he can have his own way. Hedonism obscures this natural human self-centeredness by making it appear that our desires are shaped solely by the perceived goodness of what we desire.

More significantly, hedonism oversimplifies the range of human desire by making it appear that all our desires are directed toward having pleasure and avoiding pain. This ignores the perversity of human desire, as for example, something being desirable merely because it is forbidden.

Kierkegaard's aesthetes are a varied lot. Some have discovered that certain emotions, like sorrow, sadness, and despair, have a bittersweet character, and they seek these negative feelings the way others seek sexual pleasure or money. We could argue that these aesthetes have learned to "enjoy" such things and thus are seeking pleasure after all. But this explanation requires us to posit a mysterious underlying quality of pleasure in such diverse desires as the rake's lust for immediate sexual gratification and the melancholy person's craving for bad news. The truth is that such incommensurable desires cannot be compared as if they were simply alternative means of attaining the same end. What unites the aesthetes is not that they all seek one objective good, but that they all seek to fulfill their own natural, immediate desires, whatever those may be.

The aesthetic life is the natural life of the young child. All of us begin in the aesthetic stage; many never leave it. Perhaps no one ever leaves it completely behind. We surely do not cease to have immediate desires, and they do not cease to be important to us. Nevertheless, we can see that the young child is dominated by desires in a way that the spiritually developed adult is not. Anyone who has seen a toddler throw a tantrum over some unfulfilled desire can testify to the power of that impulse. It may be of no help at all to explain to the child that it is impossible to have what he wants. The balloon is popped and cannot be put back together. "But I want it" is the child's invincible counterargument. Even the offer to get another balloon may not be good enough. "But I want *that* balloon!"

In the young child the aesthetic life is natural and, in a sense, innocent. It is true that because of original sin, the child's desires are corrupt from an early stage. Observations of young children confirm that they have selfish, aggressive, and even cruel desires along with charming and innocent wants. Kierkegaard does not think the child is really aware of these desires as evil, and he thinks children should be allowed to be children. Telling a child that he or she is bad only compounds the problem and can be a self-fulfilling prophecy. The child should not be made to feel guilty because of childlike desires.

Kierkegaard is especially cautious about how what he terms the strict ideals of Christianity should be introduced into a child's life. Reflecting on his own guilt-ridden childhood, he declares that it is "a rape, be it ever so well meant,"[2] to impose on the child the decisively Christian ideas of sin and the atonement. The very young child should be introduced to God as a loving father, and the more severe Christian concepts should be introduced as the child's conscience and spiritual capacities are developed.

As we have said, not everyone outgrows the aesthetic stage, and for many adults it becomes a way of life. In *Either-*

Or and *The Stages on Life's Way* Kierkegaard depicts a variety of aesthetic lifestyles. They all fall on a continuum between two extremes: the purely immediate aesthete on the one hand, the purely reflective aesthete on the other.

In *Either-Or* the immediate aesthete is represented by the mythical figure of Don Juan. The pseudonymous author of part I, designated as "A," writes an essay on the wonders of Mozart's operatic treatment of this figure in *Don Giovanni.* Don Juan does not write anything himself; he is too busy for that, having seduced 1,003 women "in Spain alone."[3] Don Juan is the incarnation of sensuousness and raw, immediate desire and as such could not be expected to do anything so literary and reflective as to write an essay. Nevertheless, the figure of Don Juan is important, even to the reflective aesthete. He represents what Kierkegaard calls "immediacy." Immediacy is where the aesthetic life always begins, and in a sense it is where it ends as well.

We can easily see that the ideal of life Don Juan represents—an ideal very similar to what Freud described as "the pleasure principle"—is unachievable in an unmitigated form. Regardless of the specific character of one's immediate sensuous urges, whether for sex or anything else, two daunting obstacles loom for the immediate aesthete. One lies in the objective conditions of life, the recognition of which constitutes what Freud called "the reality principle." If I live simply to satisfy my immediate urges, I will eventually be defeated by bad luck, ill-health, lack of resources, rival aesthetes, or finally death. Even more fatal to the aesthetic project of immediacy is an internal obstacle: boredom. Human beings are so constituted that living solely to satisfy immediate sensuous urges is unsatisfying in the long run. Difficult as it may be for an adolescent to imagine when in the grip of sexual passion for the first time, even sex can become stale and boring. The very thought of seducing 1,003 women is testimony to this. It is easy to imagine a real-life Don Juan as bored, and it is interesting to ask why Don Juan continually seeks out new conquests. Could it be that he restlessly seeks new victims because his encounters are never truly satisfying?

The intelligent aesthete sees the potential problems in the immediate aesthetic life and therefore does not aspire to be

Don Juan. Rather, the sophisticated aesthete, like Kierkegaard's "A," does not merely satisfy raw impulse. He has learned to vary his enjoyments and to enjoy imaginative creations. Thus the reflective aesthete is an aesthete in the more common sense of the word. You will find him at the theater, the art museum, and the opera house. The world of artistic imagination offers, not the same endless boring routine, but infinite variation. I do not have to try to be Don Juan and face the possibility of getting AIDS; I can be Don Juan vicariously when I listen to Mozart's *Don Giovanni*. When I am tired of Mozart, I can read Byron or Molière or turn from Don Juan to Faust or to painting. This is the reflective form of the aesthetic life.

The reflective aesthete has his life in what Kierkegaard calls the category of the interesting, and what better way to defeat boredom? He is less concerned with what he gets than how he gets it. This concept is beautifully captured in *Either/Or* by "The Diary of a Seducer" at the end of part I. It provides a vivid picture of the kind of seduction a reflective aesthete would pursue. In contrast to Don Juan's 1,003, the reflective seducer debauches only one woman. While Don Juan is the embodiment of raw sensuousness, the reflective seducer is almost ethereal in the cold, intellectual manner in which he plots his seduction. For the reflective seducer, the actual sexual encounter is almost insignificant, valued only for its symbolic power as proof of his superiority. He chooses a young woman of unusual intelligence and spirit and consciously sets out to develop her into a person more like himself, someone who is reflective and craves "the interesting." This is done not so much to make it possible to seduce the woman as to make the actual seduction more interesting, more of a challenge. To this end the seducer strings the whole process out at great length and devises an elaborate strategy. In the final analysis it is the process he enjoys, rather than the result; in the end the reader is not even sure whether the seduction really took place or was simply one more poetic creation of the aesthete's imagination.

The reflective form of the aesthetic life appears far more likely to be successful than the immediate form, but this appearance may be an illusion. Many problems lurk beneath the surface.

First, the aesthete has not totally escaped the objective problems of reality that threaten the immediate aesthete. It may be easier to control our pleasures when we have learned to enjoy imaginative creations, but no one can escape from real life altogether. We may watch soap operas or attend grand opera, read Harlequin novels or Shakespeare, but there comes a time when we have to face the necessities of life like preparing meals and washing dishes—assuming, of course that we have the means for dinner. It is very clear that "A" is able to play his aesthetic games partly because he is a man of some financial means, relatively untroubled by the thought of where his next meal is coming from, unscathed by serious illness or tragedy.

Second, the reflective aesthete cannot completely avoid the boredom that haunts the immediate aesthete. "A" seems to be very bored with life, to the point of being extremely "melancholy," or in today's language, depressed. The root cause is simply that humans were created to be spiritual beings. They cannot be permanently happy in the deepest sense merely by making their lives into a collection of satisfying moments. If a person has no higher purpose or meaning in life, no ideal to unify and give focus to his decisions and choices, then life becomes unsatisfying. The aimlessness of many young people in prosperous, industrialized countries testifies powerfully to this point.

In volume 2 of *Either/Or*, an older married man, who represents the ethical sphere of existence, gives a diagnosis of "A"'s melancholy. This married man, Judge William, says there comes a time in a person's life when "his immediacy is, as it were, ripened and the spirit demands a higher form in which it will apprehend itself as spirit."[4] If this development is checked and the person refuses to take responsibility for becoming what he should become, the result is melancholy. The Judge defines melancholy, in fact, as "hysteria of the spirit."[5] Melancholy happens because the "spirit does not allow itself to be mocked."[6] I do not believe Kierkegaard is suggesting that every case of modern depression fits this category, but he is claiming there is a special type of unhappiness that is the result of a person's failure to become a self in the deepest sense.

The recognition that the aesthetic life leads to melancholy, or even that it is a form of despair in the sense discussed in chapter 6, does not mean that the aesthete will necessarily reject the life he is living. It is not enough to see intellectually that "all is vanity" within the aesthetic sphere. Kierkegaard calls such an intellectual realization "existential irony." He means that the person who sees through the emptiness of the aesthetic ideal can take an ironical attitude toward what the immediate aesthete regards as ultimately important. Such an ironical attitude toward life is the boundary of the aesthetic life, the threshold of the ethical, but it is no more than that. For Kierkegaard, no existential growth occurs solely because of an intellectual insight, because there is a fundamental distinction between knowing and being, between existence and thought. It is one thing to know a lot about ethics and see its importance; it is another to be ethical. The latter requires ethical passion. It requires that one care about the ethical, and such caring cannot be reduced to an intellectual achievement.

The aesthete can in fact even learn to take refuge in melancholy. This is the secret of "A," who, as a bright intellectual, has quickly seen the futility of the aesthetic life even in its reflective form. Instead of turning away from such a life, however, "A" has learned to make his melancholy into an aesthetic object. He has, as it were, learned to enjoy his suffering. In his imagination he steps back from himself and observes the tragedy of his own life. After all, "A" is seeking the interesting, and what is more interesting than tragedy?

Ultimately the aesthete cannot be argued out of aestheticism. This is why Kierkegaard thinks it would be of no help to tack a heavy, moralistic warning onto *Either/Or.*[7] Either a person can see that the aesthetic life is perdition, or he cannot. We have seen already from our discussion of despair that such self-knowledge does not come easily and that it must be willed if it is to become a reality. We are back in the realm of self-deception and the development of the unconscious.

B. The Ethical Life: Choosing a Self

For Kierkegaard, ethical existence is the beginning of selfhood in the genuine sense. The aesthete remains at the childish level of existence, what I have termed the pre-self. As Judge William puts it in part 2 of *Either/Or,* "The aesthetic in a person is that by which he is what he is; the ethical is that by which he becomes what he becomes."[8] This means that the aesthete simply takes his personality as a given and does not recognize his responsibility to become something, to take charge of his life. In the deepest sense the aesthete does not have a self, because he does not have a unified self. His life is merely a collection of moments, and there is nothing that binds or unites those moments together and makes them into the history of a self.

From the ethical perspective, it is commitment that makes a person a self. As long as I recognize no authority or claims on my life, I am free to invent myself anew at each moment. Genuine commitment means I have staked my life to something that I recognize as having authority, as making a claim on me. Commitment in this sense can give my life coherence and unity.

The young child is incapable of choice in this profound sense, and that is why the aesthetic life is natural and normal for the child. Children very properly live in the moment, and it is touching and charming to see how passionately they can desire in one instant and abandon that desire for a new one in the next. The child may say she wants to play with a toy forever, and the expression captures the child's immediacy; but the parent is not surprised to see the child bored with the toy fifteen minutes later. What is appropriate and natural in the child is, however, a failure in the adult.

Commitment makes choice or decision in the genuine sense possible. Or, we could say that to genuinely choose or decide is to commit oneself. The aesthete makes choices of a sort. The seducer must decide which woman to seduce; the television lover must decide which program to watch. However, these choices are never binding. The seducer can always go after a different woman; the television junkie can switch channels.

To choose in the deepest sense is to regard my choice as binding me. This kind of choice is the beginning of what Kierkegaard calls "seriousness" or "earnestness," and it is the stuff out of which genuine selfhood emerges. A person who chooses, in this sense, must regard the choice as serious, and this leads to earnest self-reflection: What kind of person am I becoming by this choice? So Kierkegaard calls this inner, reflective concern "inwardness" or "subjectivity."

The ethical person cannot invent the values to which she commits herself. Her own invention could never have this sort of authority over her. Rather, the values must come from outside her. They must be transcendent. As Judge Williams puts it, I choose myself; I do not create myself.[9] The self I should become is viewed as given; my choice is only to become or not to become what I should be.

Obviously, one way of understanding values as transcendent and my ideal self as given is to see myself as created by God. Not surprisingly, Kierkegaard's examples of ethical persons are generally religious people, but he makes a distinction between the ethical and the religious life. The difference is not merely the presence or absence of conventional religious belief, either, for the ethicist may believe in God as well and take his belief very seriously.

While the ethicist may be religious in this conventional way, there are two revealing characteristics that distinguish this life from the deeper religious stage. First, the ethical person sees God abstractly as the giver of the moral law or the foundation of moral values, not as a concrete person with whom he might have dealings. The ethicist may even think of God as a person, but not as a person who might confront him as an individual as God did Abraham in the command to sacrifice Isaac. Second, the ethical person sees himself able to establish a relationship with God through his own efforts. The ethical person hears God's command to become a certain sort of self and believes he can carry it out. There is, therefore, a fundamental self-confidence in the ethical sphere that differs, as we shall see, from the characteristic attitude of religious existence as Kierkegaard sees it.

The aesthetic life was personified for Kierkegaard in the figures of Don Juan and the reflective seducer. The representative of the ethical life is appropriately enough a married man. In part 2 of *Either/Or*, Judge William gives a vigorous defense of marriage. It is a thoughtful and powerful essay, which

Kierkegaard somehow wrote even as he personally gave up the idea of marriage as a possibility for himself.

In the essay, Judge William assumes the existence of romantic love. This is a particular example of how the ethical life in general presupposes the immediate desires that are the whole content of the aesthetic life. The problem with romantic love is that it is transitory, just as the general problem with the aesthetic life is lack of continuity.

According to the Judge, marriage is the fulfillment of and not the destruction of romantic love. Ideally, when marriage is seen as an end in itself—and not betrayed by being recommended on dubious, extrinsic grounds ("it will build character," for example)—it provides a way of making love actual by giving it a history. When love is taken up by commitment, it is deepened rather than destroyed. Love itself needs the grounding of commitment if it is to endure, and the marriage ceremony is an appropriate expression of the desire of love to ground itself in a higher power. In other words, the Judge thinks that the ethical life is superior, not only ethically, but when judged by aesthetic criteria. If you want happiness, you must learn to care about something other than immediate and transitory pleasures.

The Judge's criticisms of the aesthetic life are penetrating, and his picture of the ethical life as the joyful fulfillment of duty is beautiful. However, the picture does not seem to be completely realistic. It may well be true that we ought to experience duty as the fulfillment of our immediate desires, but it is equally true that we do not usually do so. One may wonder whether even the Judge's marriage is as idyllic as he paints it. Does he never crave anything more than the domestic bliss he describes? Is there never any bickering, squabbling, or even boredom in his household? Conspicuous by its absence is the perspective of the Judge's wife. As the person who is charged with all the responsibility for child rearing, cooking, and cleaning, is her life as idyllic as he claims?

Judge William knows in one sense that people are not always ethical. He talks about the need for repentance and forgiveness. Nevertheless, there is in the end an incurable optimism about him that seems glib and even infuriating. In one of his letters to "A" he stresses the power of a good woman to change a man: "Of a hundred men who go astray in the world ninety-nine are saved by women and one by immediate divine grace."[10] Even if we ignore the obviously male perspective of this quote, it is striking in that it assumes that no one is ultimately lost.

The Judge recognizes correctly that the aesthetic life is despair. His prescription, however, is for the aesthete to despair. That is, the aesthete must consciously despair of the immediate desires that constitute his life and begin to recognize his spiritual character. The aesthete must take responsibility for being the despairing person he is and thereby become the sort of person who can choose to be someone. The question is whether it is really possible to do this. Can a human being collect himself and become the self he ought to be through an act of will?

Johannes Climacus, the pseudonymous author of *Concluding Unscientific Postscript*, suggests in a review of *Either/Or* that there are problems the Judge has not really faced. "I think that the Judge, supposing I could get hold of him and whisper a little secret in his ear, will concede that there are difficulties he did not take into account."[11]

The problem with the ethical life is described more bluntly by another pseudonymous writer, Johannes de Silentio, in *Fear and Trembling*. "As soon as sin emerges, ethics founders precisely on repentance; for repentance is the highest ethical expression, but precisely as such it is the deepest ethical self-contradiction."[12] The person who is most deeply ethical is the very person who recognizes how far from being truly ethical he is. The Judge tells the aesthete to despair actively in the sense of choosing to take responsibility for being a despairer. The religious person wonders whether such despair is profound enough. Can I really despair of myself by myself? And if I can, is it possible to recover from such despair by myself? Such questions are the foundation of the religious life.

C. The Religious Life: Recovering the Self

Though Kierkegaard talks about the stages on life's way, it is easy to see why he does not assign these stages to particular ages. The aesthetic life is universal in the young child, and we can see the ethical stage as natural to the young adolescent who is learning to choose and to take responsibility for choices. But there are many adults who remain childish in the aesthetic sense and perhaps many children who are reflective enough to begin to live ethically at an early age. The growth of a self is a spiritual process that cannot be assigned to a particular age. It occurs at different times in people, if it occurs at all.

For a person to be religious in the Kierkegaardian sense requires a certain maturity. Though the foundations of the religious life are surely formed at a very early age, its full expression requires some experience. The experiences in question are heavily ethical in character, for Kierkegaard sees the religious life as growing out of the ethical life. This does not mean a person must spend a long period of time in the ethical sphere before he can begin to live religiously, but it does mean he must have some awareness of the meaning and significance of ethical concepts. Kierkegaard says explicitly that *conscience* is what constitutes the relationship to God (p. 124).

Kierkegaard's view of the relation between the ethical and the religious life is complex. On the one hand, he does not want to reduce the religious life to ethical striving, as the liberal theologians who were his contemporaries were trying to do. The religious life has its own inner dynamic and is by no means simply intensified ethical striving. In fact, Kierkegaard says the ethical life can become the enemy of the religious life, as ethical striving can be a mask for pride and an expression of the drive for autonomy that he sees as the heart of sinfulness. On the other hand, the religious life is also inconceivable as totally divorced from the ethical life. The ethical ideals reappear within the religious sphere in a transformed manner. As the ethical person argues that the goals of the aesthetic life are more adequately realized within the ethical life, so the religious person argues that the ideals of the ethical life are more adequately realized within a religious life, in which the person gives up his self-confident autonomy and learns to trust wholly in God.

Johannes de Silentio, the pseudonymous author of *Fear*

and Trembling, uses Abraham as his paradigm of the religious person. Abraham showed his faith in his willingness to sacrifice Isaac. This action cannot be explained or justified solely in ethical terms; it was an action whereby Abraham showed his supreme trust in God. It is true that God did not require the sacrifice, but Abraham presumably did not know that beforehand.

There is little question that Kierkegaard saw the Abraham story as reiterated in his own life. He believed God had asked him to sacrifice marriage and his beloved Regine just as Abraham had been asked to sacrifice Isaac. Thus the illustrative religious figure who corresponds to the aesthetic seducer and the ethical married man is the person who has chosen voluntary celibacy for the sake of the kingdom of God. This does not mean, of course, that all religious persons must be celibate, but it symbolizes the willingness of the truly religious person to give up any finite commitment for the sake of the relationship to God.

The point of *Fear and Trembling* is not, as some have thought, to explore the question whether God might require us to do some terrible, immoral action. The point is rather that the greatness of Abraham cannot be understood in purely ethical terms. Either there is something more to the religious life than moral striving, or else "Abraham is lost."[13]

Why should we care if there is more to life than moral striving? The person who has discovered genuine moral guilt cares, because if there is nothing more to life than ethical striving, all is lost. Such profoundly religious notions as forgiveness and atonement are simply not understandable in purely moral terms. A wholly ethical Abraham would be admired, but "it is one thing to be admired; it is another thing to be a guiding star which saves the anguished."[14]

Since the foundation of the religious life is a very unpleasant discovery about oneself, it is not surprising that Kierkegaard believed that genuinely religious persons were rare in educated, middle-class Danish circles, though almost everyone he knew was religious and even "Christian" in a conventional way. Though Kierkegaard was not an elitist and was careful to recognize the possibility that real faith was common among the poor and uneducated, he felt that too many of his peers had substituted an intellectual understanding of Christianity for actually existing as a Christian. Thus he discovered his vocation of being a missionary to Christendom, of helping people who assumed they were already Christians come to some understanding of what genuine Christianity is all about.

To help achieve this end, Kierkegaard distinguishes two forms of the religious life, termed "religiousness A" and "religiousness B," in *Concluding Unscientific Postscript*. He describes religiousness A as a natural religiosity. It is, one might say, the kind of religiousness that is possible merely by virtue of God's general revelation of himself. It does not rest on any transcendent revelation, but only on the knowledge of God that is present within or "immanent to" human consciousness.

Religiousness A can come to an awareness of God and can recognize that the relationship to God is more important than anything else. Its task is to develop "an absolute relation to the absolute; a relative relation to the relative."[15] This requires what Kierkegaard calls "resignation," a willingness to give up the finite for the sake of the infinite. However, as humans we soon discover that we are not willing to do this; we are "trapped in immediacy." Hence the essence of the religious life turns out to be suffering, a dying to self that is necessary if God is to be God.[16] But the honest religious person comes to see that this is not possible either. Thus the "decisive" expression for the religious life turns out to be guilt.[17] The religious person recognizes himself as guilty, not just of this or that moral infraction, but guilty before God.

The problem for the natural religious life is dealing with guilt. Confronting guilt is so difficult that we are naturally tempted to sweep it under the rug or deny that it exists. The best the natural religious life can do here is to respond in repentance and hope that guilt can be resolved, but there is always a danger that the person will be paralyzed by the problem.

One form of this paralysis is the kind of life Kierkegaard calls "humor."[18] (The word is here used as a technical term; in the more ordinary sense of the term Kierkegaard saw humor as an element in the Christian life.) Humor is a kind of boundary zone of religious existence, just as irony is a kind of boundary zone for ethical existence. The humorist is the person who has learned to smile at life. He has seen the problem of guilt, the humoristic contradiction between the ideals we humans recognize and our feeble progress toward those ideals. The humorist thinks we can smile at that contradiction because he believes that at bottom we are all "saved." "We all get equally far," says the humorist. But in a sense we all get nowhere, and the humorist smiles at the differences between one human being's efforts and another's. For the humorist, we can relax a little because essentially we all possess God already, no matter what we do.[19] "I'm okay, and you're okay."

Kierkegaard says this humoristic view of life is very close to Christianity. Indeed, I believe that many so-called Christian theologians today, as well as some psychologists, have confused this life-view with Christianity. Kierkegaard sees a vast difference between them. The humorist is described as someone who has acquired a knowledge of Christian concepts without understanding these existentially.[20] That is, the humorist has heard the good news of Christianity, of grace and forgiveness, of a solution to the problem of guilt. But he has failed to see that this grace and forgiveness are not eternal possessions that all human beings automatically own, but are something only Jesus Christ can give.

The religiousness that recognizes the centrality of a relationship with Christ is, of course, Christian faith. This is what is called religiousness B in *Postscript*. It is also described as "transcendent" religiousness, because in contrast to the immanence of religiousness A, the knowledge of God here comes through a transcendent revelation.

Christianity marks the end of the road for autonomy and the recovery of total dependence on God. Religiousness A recognizes the arrogant self-confidence of the ethical life, yet it assumes that a person can come to know God and relate to him through individual efforts. To become a Christian I must recognize my inability to know God through my own reasoning. I can only know God as he reveals himself to me in Jesus Christ, who is a historical figure and not a mythical ideal latent in my consciousness.

Kierkegaard insists that the Incarnation is opaque to human reason, a paradox that undermines any claim of philosophers or brilliant minds to have an advantage when it comes to the knowledge of God. When the task is to recognize the limits of our reason and humbly accept God's revelation, we are all on equal footing. If reason cannot accept its limits, it will naturally be offended by the gospel, which in the final analysis is a rebuke to our self-sufficiency.[21] Our task is not to understand how God could become a human being, but how we become followers of Jesus. Faith is described as a "leap," since it requires a choice, but strictly speaking, I cannot decide to have faith in Jesus. That faith must be created in me by God himself. All I can decide to do is to recognize the limits God has revealed to me.[22]

For Kierkegaard, Jesus must be seen as both "the pattern" and "the redeemer."[23] As the Son of God in human form, Jesus teaches me what human life was meant to be and how far from that life I am. In discovering my sinfulness I also discover my need for a savior. Thus Jesus offers himself as the atonement for sin, the one who reconciles me to God. Through the love and forgiveness he extends I am again strengthened to view Jesus as the pattern, to begin to follow him and not merely to admire him. The attempt to follow will once more bring a humbling recognition of my need for forgiveness, and so it goes, in an ongoing process of growth.

The real follower of Jesus does not merely accept intellectually the proposition that Jesus is God, but actually accepts Jesus as Lord. We can see now why Kierkegaard was so critical of "Christendom," which assumed that everyone in Denmark (or any other "Christian" country) is a Christian by virtue of baptism or by virtue of not being a Muslim or a Buddhist.

Genuine Christianity is a vigorous, tough-minded solution to the problems of human existence. Christian psychology can play a vital role in helping to reintroduce Christianity into Christendom, because if we do not understand the problems of human existence, we cannot understand how Christianity could be a solution. To a follower of Jesus Christ, all the rich insights into despair and faith as its cure acquire concrete meaning. As Jesus' follower I can begin to rest transparently "in the power which formed the self." That power is no longer an abstraction; it is a living reality that relativizes every other power that promises a sure foundation for selfhood.

Notes

1. Søren Kierkegaard, *Either/Or*, vol. 1, ed. and trans. Howard V. Hong and Edna H. Hong (Princeton: Princeton University Press, 1987), 31.

2. Søren Kierkegaard, *Concluding Unscientific Postscript*, trans. David Swenson and Walter Lowrie (Princeton: Princeton University Press, 1968), 524.

3. Kierkegaard, *Either/Or*, 1:91.

4. Ibid. The translation used in this case and some of the following references is the old one by Walter Lowrie (Princeton: Princeton University Press, 1972), 2:193.

5. Kierkegaard, *Either/Or*, 2:193 (Lowrie translation).

6. Ibid., 2:208.

7. See Kierkegaard, *Concluding Unscientific Postscript*, 263–64.

8. Kierkegaard, *Either/Or*, 2:178 (Hong translation modified by me in this case).

9. Ibid., 2:215 (Hong translation).

10. Ibid., 2:207.

11. Kierkegaard, *Concluding Unscientific Postscript*, 161.

12. Søren Kierkegaard, *Fear and Trembling*, ed. and trans. Howard V. Hong and Edna H. Hong (Princeton: Princeton University Press, 1983), 98n.

13. Ibid., 81.

14. Ibid., 21.

15. Kierkegaard, *Concluding Unscientific Postscript*, 347.

16. Ibid., 386–468.

17. Ibid., 468–69.

18. For a more detailed account of Kierkegaard's view of humor, both in this technical sense and in the more ordinary sense, see my "Kierkegaard's View of Humor: Must Christians Always Be Solemn?" *Faith and Philosophy* 4, no. 2 (1987): 176–86.

19. See Kierkegaard, *Concluding Unscientific Postscript*, 400–402.

20. Ibid., 243.

21. These themes are most prominently developed in *Philosophical Fragments*, ed. and trans. Howard V. Hong and Edna H. Hong (Princeton: Princeton University Press, 1985).

22. See chapter 4 of *Philosophical Fragments*.

23. These themes are displayed most clearly in *Training in Christianity*, trans. Walter Lowrie (Princeton: Princeton University Press, 1941), particularly selections 232 and 270 in the "edifying discourse," "The Woman That Was a Sinner," published with *Training in Christianity*.

CHAPTER 8

Kierkegaard as Therapist: Applying Psychology

Kierkegaard was obviously not a therapist in the contemporary sense. And since I am not a therapist or professional counselor, it would be fruitless for me to attempt to develop a full-blown system of therapy out of Kierkegaard's writings. Such a system would be woefully incomplete because there are many kinds of psychological difficulties Kierkegaard does not address. Moreover, given my lack of experience, it would be presumptuous and highly speculative for me to try to address some of those problems, with or without Kierkegaard's help.

Nevertheless, I believe that the psychological insights I have tried to explain in the previous chapters have some interesting practical implications for the clinical psychologist. They also have implications for people in other fields. For example, the developmental theory of the stages has some clear implications for Christian education and nurture. If Kierkegaard's views here are close to the truth, then the very young child, whose life is still largely aesthetic and immediate, should be introduced to those aspects of Christianity that correspond to her immediate needs. She should be taught about a God who loves her and cares for her. As the child moves into the ethical stage, it is appropriate to begin to emphasize the ideals of goodness, justice, and love that God embodies and expects us to emulate. The older child or adolescent who has some experience with the struggle to do this is ready to begin to understand the Christian doctrines of the atonement and sanctification and the stricter demands of following Christ.

This does not mean that the child must have moved through these stages before she can think of herself as a Christian, a follower of Jesus. Rather, her understanding of what it means to be a follower of Jesus will naturally change over time. This is one of the more obvious applications of Kierkegaard's theory of the stages to Christian nurture, but there are many others. I shall try to discuss several, focusing particularly on the therapeutic situation in the last part of this chapter.

Psychology and Evangelism

In the first chapter I recounted Kierkegaard's understanding of himself as a missionary to a supposedly Christian land, charged with the task of "reintroducing Christianity into Christendom." I pointed out that Kierkegaard sees psychology as playing a key role in his task, since a mature understanding of what it means to live or exist as a human being is a precondition for understanding Christianity in the most decisive sense. We can now ask how psychology can best fulfill its role.

In general, what Kierkegaard wants for his contemporaries (and later readers) is that they come to an understanding of their spiritual nature and spiritual condition. In other words, he would like them to appropriate, in a personal and not just academic way, the insights we have explored in chapters 3 through 7. The question remains as to how this task is best accomplished.

Kierkegaard believed in approaching the task *indirectly.* It is no good thundering at people or preaching to them from a superior position; nor will it do much good simply to lay out a theory of human development for them. Thundering at them from on high will only make them defensive and more resistant to insight; laying out an academic theory for them may only bolster one of the worst tendencies of the modern age, intellectualism.

Intellectualism, to Kierkegaard's mind, is just another

version of the aesthetic life. The intellectualist is someone who thinks we become what we should be as human beings by knowing the right facts or having the right objective thoughts. The intellectual confuses being an ethical person with knowing a lot about ethical theory; he thinks he is a person of faith merely because he knows a lot of theology, or a person of wisdom because he has a lot of scientific knowledge. The intellectualist, however much he may look different from the Seducer in *Either/Or*, is a form of aesthete in the final analysis because he uses his intellectual powers to evade the responsible choices that constitute genuine human existence. Instead of choosing, the intellectualist puts life at a distance by objectifying every issue into an interesting exercise for thought.

Kierkegaard's indirect method for helping his contemporaries is modeled on Socrates. Socrates described himself as a midwife, who had no wisdom of his own to impart but saw it as his task to help others give birth to their own ideas. In this view Socrates did not see himself as superior to anyone else, but was essentially equal to those he hoped to teach.

Consistent with this stance, Socrates adopted a method of critical questioning. When he encountered a politician who claimed to know what was right and just, he did not begin by telling the fellow he was wrong and proceeding to give him a better theory. Rather, he took the person's word for it and, on the assumption that the politician did indeed know about justice, began to question him. The end result, of course, was that the politician got an inkling that he did not understand what he was talking about. He was reduced from "knowledge" to ignorance, but in recognizing his ignorance lay the beginning of wisdom. Socrates' image of a midwife could be described as *the maieutic ideal*, the term "maieutic" being drawn from the Greek word for a midwife.

Kierkegaard believed strongly in the maieutic ideal. He attempted to take a Socratic standpoint toward a society in which it was assumed "we are all Christians." Instead of directly attacking the illusion by claiming that other people were not true Christians, Kierkegaard adopted the ironical method of taking other people at their word, accepting their illusion as "good money." He then engaged them in a Socratic manner. Instead of claiming to be a superior Christian, he went so far as to declare that he was perhaps the only one in Denmark who was not a Christian. He was still in the process of *becoming* a Christian, still *on the way.* No doubt his Christian contemporaries had already achieved the spiritual state Kierkegaard believed God was still helping him to attain, and therefore they could enlighten him, much as Athenian politicians were supposed to be able to enlighten Socrates!

Kierkegaard used a variety of strategies to attempt to engage his contemporaries Socratically. We noted in chapter 7 the role of the pseudonyms, who were supposed to function as literary mirrors to his contemporaries. Kierkegaard also made extensive use of irony and humor, which function, it will be recalled, as boundary zones along the stages of life's way and can thereby be a prelude to growth. For those who were spiritually open, he wrote a long series of edifying discourses, which begin with a kind of natural religiousness and finally become clearly and decisively Christian. In all this his aim was to develop the kind of inwardness or subjectivity which is prerequisite to being a serious Christian.

This inwardness consists of "passion," which is a key term in Kierkegaard's writings. Passion is not merely a momentary feeling, an external force that sweeps a person out of control, as in "he shot her in a fit of passion." Such momentary emotions are purely aesthetic for Kierkegaard. The truly significant passions are those enduring concerns that give shape and unity to a person's life. The distinction between the aesthetic and the ethical life is that the ethical person has begun to develop some passions, which are more than the momentary impulses that shape the aesthete. The ethical person cares about such things as kindness and gratitude, fairness and fidelity. The religious life, in turn, is a matter of acquiring new passions, particularly such virtues as faith, hope, and love.

Since human beings are free, spiritual beings, there are no techniques that are guaranteed to work in helping others to develop passions. Ultimately the person must choose. And there are strict limits to the Socratic method, since the distinctively Christian virtues can only be developed by God himself when he encounters us in Jesus Christ. All the Socratic gadfly can do is seek to help others develop the kind of self-concern that will allow them to engage the Christian gospel.

Still, there is a kind of maieutic ideal that is valid even within the distinctively Christian sphere because it is truly God who creates faith in the individual. The most I can do through my witness is to be a channel, an occasion for God to meet other people; so a kind of Socratic equality with no room for superiority on my part is still valid for the Christian. Socratic humility is deepened and not abolished by the Christian revelation.

To me there is little question that Kierkegaard's situation is still with us. We are more than ever in need of missionaries to Christendom. If Kierkegaard were alive today, he would doubtless have new, creative ideas for dealing with the situation, and he certainly would urge us to use our creativity to develop new strategies for encountering our contemporaries. Some of his strategies will seem worthwhile—particularly the use of literature to engage and hold up a mirror to people and the use of irony and humor to expose the illusions that grip us.

I also think Kierkegaard is right in warning us not to allow the modern unbeliever to get away with his claim that his difficulties with Christianity are purely intellectual. If people in "modern" or "post-modern" society have trouble developing Christian faith, the reason may not be at all that we are too intelligent or learned to believe as people of past ages did. The problem may lie in our constricted understanding of what our essential task is as human beings and our impoverished attempts to become selves. It is not that we are too intelligent and learned to become Christians, but that we have deceived ourselves into thinking that intellectual achievements are what human life is all about.

Incarnational Therapy: Spiritual Health and Mental Health

Kierkegaard would reject any claim that a person is always responsible for his psychological problems. Doubtless there is a sense in which psychological problems are due to sin, since all human suffering can in one way or another be traced to sin. However, this by no means implies that the problems of a particular person are caused by his sinfulness. Many psychological problems, including some of Kierkegaard's own, are caused by the sins of other people. Other psychological problems are undoubtedly caused by physiological factors and therefore must be understood as rooted in the fallenness of the physical universe, which is in some way a consequence of the fall of the race as a whole. Yet this does not imply that people who suffer from physical ailments are being punished for their individual sins.

Nevertheless, though not all psychological problems are due to a person's spiritual condition, Kierkegaard believed some such conditions are spiritual in origin and require a spiritual cure. Also, other conditions not traceable to spiritual causes may be successfully approached from a spiritual perspective—that is, they can be alleviated through faith, the state in which the individual rests transparently in God.

We saw in chapter 5 how sin, the break in the God-relationship, causes a variety of distortions in the personality. Instead of the creative balance between the infinite and the finite, the eternal and the temporal, people find themselves mired in spiritless fatalism or lost in a fantasyland of ideals that have no relation to concrete reality. Faith is the cure that enables a person to accept the concrete being he is, warts and all, and to move toward becoming the ideal person God has created him to be, since for God all things are possible. The person who stands before God in faith can begin to overcome the self-deception that is endemic to human life. If I can trustingly reveal myself to God, I have no reason to hide the truth from myself or ultimately from other humans as well.

Humans cannot gain this faith through philosophical thinking or moral striving. It is created in people solely through an encounter with God as he has revealed himself in Jesus. In Jesus I learn what God is like and what I am supposed to be like. In Jesus I discover how far from God and my true self I am. In Jesus I discover God's love in forgiving and atoning for my sin. In Jesus I discover the possibility of a new beginning as I stake my identity on him and commit myself to being his follower.

Kierkegaard's view of the person has some significant

implications for contemporary psychotherapies. These psychotherapies usually involve three elements, emphasized to varying degrees according to the particular school of therapy. These elements are insight, action, and relationship. Freudian approaches tend to emphasize insight; cognitive-behavioral approaches, action; and Rogerian or client-centered approaches, the importance of a loving, healing relationship. Yet all these elements are present in each school. Freudian therapists clearly recognize the importance of relationship when they talk about the phenomenon of transference. Rogerian therapists may see the relationship as a means for the client to gain insight. Behavioral-cognitive therapists also recognize the importance of insight and understand the importance of a good therapeutic relationship. Still, significant differences in emphasis remain.

Kierkegaardian thought implies that Christian faith can contribute to all three of these elements. It is unfortunate that Kierkegaard's reputation as the father of existentialism has led many to the assumption that his thinking is only relevant to existential psychology. This is far from the case. To see this, let us look briefly at each of the approaches to therapy we have mentioned.

Dynamic approaches to therapy emphasize the role of the unconscious and often focus on relationships and events from early childhood. It is clear that Kierkegaard would not want a dynamic therapist to view me merely as a helpless victim of the past. His focus would be on the meaning my past can have as I project my ideals into the future. Yet he would agree with the dynamic therapist that gaining insight into the unconscious is of the utmost importance. Much of the story of human development as told by dynamic therapists—especially objects-relations theorists—Kierkegaard can accept, at least as an adequate account of the emergence of the pre-self. What he can add to the story is the central role an unconscious awareness of God plays in the development of the mature self and the central role the repression of this knowledge plays in the development of the dynamic unconscious. Kierkegaard also offers hints about the spiritual resources Christianity provides for the healing of the unconscious. He wants us to take seriously the idea that an encounter with Jesus Christ can lead to insight into who I am and who I should be.

Kierkegaard also has much to offer the cognitive-behavioral therapist. Cognitive-behavioral therapy rightly understands the importance of patterns of thinking and action in human living. Kierkegaard's insights suggest ways of thinking about such things as anxiety and suffering that differ radically from the analysis found in secular forms of cognitive-behavioral therapy. Since I said quite a bit about anxiety in chapter 4, I will say just a bit about suffering at this point. While he is not oblivious to the pain of suffering, Kierkegaard believes that no view of human life can be taken seriously that does not see some positive potential in suffering. Distinctions must be made, of course, between different kinds of suffering. There is the suffering bound up with learning to "die to self" as the person learns what it really means to let God be absolute and thus take priority over every finite good in life. There is the voluntary suffering Christians risk whenever they decide to openly follow Christ and come into conflict with worldly values. There is suffering that must simply be patiently endured as a person struggles to accept a seemingly pointless situation as one that can be nevertheless referred to God.

The issue of suffering is just an illustration of the way a distinctively Christian cognitive therapist might analyze events in a person's life from a spiritual context. All kinds of psychological problems such as phobias and neuroses may turn out to have spiritual components that lend themselves to this kind of understanding. Nor should the matter of behavior be ignored. The behavioral therapist may rightly challenge people to express their verbal commitments in action and thereby make them real. Kierkegaard wants to emphasize that the self is formed through its choices, and behavioral "homework" is a natural expression of this insight. Nor should the behavioral therapist be shy about the need for Christian obedience in clients who say they are Christians, since a serious encounter with Jesus Christ can lead to the kind of personal growth that heals a variety of spiritually related psychological problems.

Kierkegaard's insights are hardly alien to the client-centered therapist either. This therapist can see himself as a midwife who helps the client to gain a sense of the grace and forgiveness of God. The therapist can model that acceptance and forgiveness without in any way making it appear that such love implies a sloppy relativism indifferent to the demands of justice and righteousness. The therapist can help make possible a serious encounter with Jesus Christ that can lead to a healing relationship, as I experience a sense of being accepted, forgiven, and loved unconditionally, with no need to earn or deserve the possibilities offered to me.

This means, I think, that for problems which can be successfully attacked by spiritual growth, the Christian therapist, regardless of his school, should recognize the power of Christian faith. If human psychological health is inextricably tied to spiritual health, then it is impossible for the Christian therapist to function in a value-neutral way, as if a person's God-relationship were a peripheral fact with no significant consequences. Everyone needs the gospel to become spiritually whole, but there are people who need to hear and respond to the gospel even to become psychologically whole.

This does not mean that faith is a magical cure-all for every psychological problem. We have said there are many problems that may be unrelated to spiritual growth. There may even be, because of our fallenness, problems that are caused by spiritual growth. Kierkegaard himself thinks there is a special kind of psychological suffering that is the result of a spiritual trial, a kind of test that only people who are growing spiritually undergo.[1] A spiritual trial is a form of temptation in which a person who is being asked by God to do something special is tempted to relapse into a conventional ethical life. Even for problems that can be treated spiritually, Kierkegaard's view does not imply that these problems will vanish immediately when a person becomes a Christian. Rather, Kierkegaard stresses that Christian faith is a process and that spiritual growth is a slow undertaking as God attempts to develop his character within us.

Still, the range of problems that may be open to spiritual development may be wider than we might think at first. An illustration is my struggle with an airplane phobia. Phobias would seem to be the least spiritual type of psychological problem; it is well known that phobias are often created by traumatic experiences and that they are often successfully treated by behavioral techniques such as systematic desensitization.

My phobia was brought on by a traumatic flight. I have benefited from the relaxation techniques and other strategies recommended by contemporary therapists. But in dealing with my phobia I discovered a spiritual component. I was afraid to fly on an airplane in part because of a lack of faith in God. I did not trust God to take care of my family if something should happen to me. I did not trust God to providentially direct my own life. I could not accept the truth that ultimately it is God who must decide when my course on this earth is run.

I confess that I am still nervous on airplanes, but I have become a "frequent flier" and find flying relatively painless now. When I feel anxious and afraid, I consider it an opportunity to recommit my life and loved ones to God, a chance to relearn hard-earned lessons. The anxiety I do feel I commit to God. If he chooses not to totally remove my fear of flying, he must have a purpose in doing so, and I must trust him to help me deal with the fear.

In saying that there can be a positive relationship between spiritual health and mental health, I am using the term "mental health" in a special, religious sense. For the Christian psychotherapist, mental health cannot be defined in a neutral or value-free way because the Christian faith implies a definite view of what mental health is.

Following Kierkegaard's lead, we can say that mental health is the state of the person who is receiving new life from God and learning to be the self God has created him to be. The aesthete would consider mental health a matter of satisfying as many immediate desires as possible. The legalistic ethicist would consider it a matter of abiding by a certain ideal of behavior. But the Christian holds to a spiritual view of mental health, involving a new scale of values in which pleasure is not the highest good. Indeed, the Christian who follows Jesus may even choose to suffer at times and will be prepared to accept unavoidable suffering with gratitude from the hand of a loving God. The Christian is not concerned with balancing pleasure and pain, but in becoming the kind of person God intends him to be.

Christianity teaches that the life emerging from the relationship to God is characterized by joyfulness. Kierkegaard goes so far as to say that in some respects the life of faith is a return to the immediacy of the aesthetic life, a "higher immediacy."[2] That is, the Christian life involves a recovery of the spontaneity and innocence of the child. In faith we are truly "born again," and those who enter the kingdom of God have become "like little children." But this immediacy is a higher immediacy, gained by dying to the earthly immediacy with Christ and living through the power of Christ's resurrection.

Ultimately the source of the insight, action, and relationship that can heal is the incarnate Jesus Christ. The Christian therapist who has experienced that healing relationship, who has gained insight into himself, and who is actively following Christ can hope to be an agent for the spiritual healing of others by pointing others to Christ. Through the relationship the therapist can be a channel for God's love to the person with problems and can try to help a person who has never experienced love understand what God is like. The therapist can analyze the person's spiritual situation if the person is willing to receive such insights. The therapist can help the person to see what a real commitment to Christ might require in the way of action.

Incarnational Psychotherapy and the Maieutic Ideal

A willingness to claim that Christian faith itself provides resources for healing will require a certain boldness on the part of Christian therapists and counselors. Such a view is especially difficult for those who may work in secular institutions such as hospitals, public schools, and mental health centers. It also poses problems for some "third-party payment" situations, where the third party may insist on religious neutrality.

I have no easy answers to offer people in these situations, except to note that secular forms of psychotherapy are not, as they often claim to be, value-neutral or religiously neutral. While fighting to have this insight recognized, Christian therapists and counselors may have to limit themselves to working with problems and issues that can be successfully tackled independently of the spiritual core of the personality, or rest content with less than optimum treatments for problems that are genuinely spiritual.

However, even therapists who are free of such constraints may wonder if it is right to rely on Christianity in such a direct manner. Specifically they may wonder if this view of therapy sufficiently respects the freedom and autonomy of the client. Am I being fully honest with a client who comes to me with a phobia if I witness to that client? Did he come for therapy, or preaching? If I pray with a client, am I stepping out of my role as therapist?

The incarnational psychotherapist must be open about what he or she is up to. There should be no attempt to disguise what is being offered. However, the Christian psychotherapist who wishes to follow Kierkegaard's perspective would still show respect for the autonomy and freedom of the client. This is evident if we compare the incarnational therapist we have described with a Rogerian therapist.

We have seen that Kierkegaard considers the maieutic ideal still valid for the Christian. The form of psychotherapy that has perhaps taken that ideal most seriously is Rogerian, or client-centered, therapy. The Rogerian therapist takes on the role of midwife, or in more contemporary language, facilitator, for the growth of others. Like Socrates, Carl Rogers assumes that the truth is present within each person and must therefore be discovered by that person.

Now, the Christian psychotherapist is in one sense most unlike the Rogerian, on Kierkegaard's view. Far from assuming that the person has the truth already present within him, the Christian psychotherapist assumes that the truth must be brought by God incarnate in Jesus and so the person must encounter Jesus to be fully whole. But let us not assume that a witness to Christ violates the maieutic ideal; instead, we must look more closely at the character of an encounter with the gospel.

When God became man, he did so in the form of a poor, outwardly insignificant individual. The form of God's revelation to us is most important. Without presuming to be able to say why God acted as he did, says Kierkegaard, we can nonetheless see part of what God accomplished by coming to us as he did. Though it is a very imperfect analogy, Kierkegaard asks us to reflect on the old fairy tale of the mighty king who falls in love with a simple peasant.[3] How should he woo her? If he orders her to marry him under threat of punishment and frightens her with a display of royal military might, the girl will doubtless comply, but he will not have won her love. If he brings her to the palace and dazzles her with riches and splendors, he may succeed in making her happy in her own mind and getting her to agree to be his bride, but he could never know whether she really cared for him rather than his riches and splendors. So what must the king do? He must don a disguise and woo her incognito. He must go to her and enter her world.

That is, of course, what God has done in Jesus—only more so, because the Incarnation is not merely a disguise. Jesus truly entered our world and took on our condition. When God chose to reveal himself, he could have frightened us into compliance with his will through a display of his power. He could have dazzled us with pleasures and ecstasies beyond our present experience. However, if he did those things he would not have revealed himself as he truly is—pure, self-giving love—and he would not have won our devotion to his true self. We would fear the omnipotent enforcer or love the celestial sugar daddy, but we would not love God as God. In coming to us in the way he did, God respects our freedom. He treats us as spiritual beings who can choose to relate to him or not.

This condition establishes sharp limits to what one human being can be for another. No Christian should dare to try to be for another what not even God has allowed himself to be. There is a sense, then, in which God himself respects the maieutic ideal. This means that the Christian who witnesses to another should never use deceit, manipulation, or heavy-handed pressure.

Yet this also implies that the Christian can boldly witness to another without fear that this witness in itself is a threat to the autonomy of the other. The nature of God's incarnation ensures this. When I point another person to Jesus, I am pointing to the humble servant, not the divine enforcer or the celestial sugar daddy. It is God himself who must create faith in the other, and I can trust God to respect the dignity of his creation.

In *Works of Love*, Kierkegaard describes the role of the Christian as a maieutic lover. Love builds up or edifies the other by presupposing that love is present in the other as the ground or foundation of the personality.[4] Love believes in the other and always tries to discover a mitigating explanation of the other's behavior or put the most loving interpretation possible on his actions.[5] Love always has hope for the other,[6] unselfishly seeks the other's good,[7] and seeks to forgive those who have wronged it.[8] Love abides, because it is rooted in eternity, not merely in time.[9]

In all these works, love is humble. Even when it meets opposition, love must not take the standpoint of victor, but rather seek reconciliation with the other.[10] Kierkegaard imagines that in helping another maieutically to become himself, Socrates expresses ironical satisfaction and assumes a position of superiority: "Now he stands alone . . . with my help."[11] The Rogerian therapist might easily say the same thing. But the Christian therapist must take a different standpoint. She must say, "Every human being stands alone—by God's help."[12] She must therefore say the same thing about herself. Consequently there is no room for pride or superiority. The maieutic ideal is fully respected between one human being and another. Because both owe everything to God, there is essential equality.

Even more significantly, because both owe everything to God, neither truly stands alone. Both stand with God and therefore they stand together. We have seen that Kierkegaard's view of the self is thoroughly relational. In chapter 3 we emphasized how relations to others can be pathological substitutes for the relation to God. But the person who stands before God in faith is not an isolated individual. She stands with God and together with her brothers and sisters in love, including those who are sharing her experience of God's love and those she would like to introduce to that experience.

For Kierkegaard, the goal of selfhood is to make true community possible. Because of his polemics against the crowd and the evils of mass society, Kierkegaard is often stereotyped as someone who glorified a type of radical individualism. Nothing could be further from the truth. Rather, the Christian ideal is "the transfigured rendering of that which the politician has thought of in his happiest moment, if so be that he truly loves what it is to be a man, and loves people really."[13]

It follows from this that Christian therapy must also be placed in the context of community. The goal is not to build solitary individuals, but individuals in community.

Kierkegaard saw a decadent Christendom that was more a part of the problem than the solution in perpetuating the illusion that we are all Christians. As a consequence, I think, he did not adequately envision the way the church as a community can contribute toward these goals. I believe, however, that a faithful church, a community of the committed, is ultimately the context where Kierkegaard's ideals can best be realized. Such a community would provide the best context for Christian healers, professional and lay. Without in any way disparaging the knowledge or skills of the professional therapist, Kierkegaard would have us recognize that the people of faith have resources that do indeed make them competent to counsel.

Notes

1. See Kierkegaard's *Concluding Unscientific Postscript*, trans. David Swenson and Walter Lowrie (Princeton: Princeton University Press, 1968), 410–12.

2. Ibid., 310n.

3. The following section draws on chapter 2 of *Philosophical Fragments*, ed. and trans. Howard V. Hong and Edna H. Hong (Princeton: Princeton University Press, 1985).

4. Søren Kierkegaard, *Works of Love*, trans. Howard V. Hong and Edna H. Hong (New York: Harper & Row, 1962), 199–212.

5. Ibid., 213–30.

6. Ibid., 231–46.

7. Ibid., 247–60.

8. Ibid., 261–78.

9. Ibid., 279–91.

10. Ibid., 306–310.

11. Ibid., 258.

12. Ibid., 259.

13. Søren Kierkegaard, "The Individual," published with *The Point of View for My Work as an Author*, trans. Walter Lowrie (New York: Harper & Row, 1962), 107.

For Further Reading

One aim of this book is to increase interest in Kierkegaard among Christian psychologists, pastors, and counselors. As an aid to those who are motivated to read Kierkegaard on their own, I provide here a brief annotated bibliography. I have included only the major works of Kierkegaard relevant to these issues, all of which are discussed at some point in the text. I also include a couple of secondary sources that provide good starting points to that literature. A fairly complete bibliography on Kierkegaard can be found in Francis Lapointe, *Søren Kierkegaard and His Critics* (Westport, Conn.: Greenwood Press, 1980).

Books by Kierkegaard

The Concept of Anxiety, translated by Reidar Thomte (Princeton: Princeton University Press, 1980). Though one of the more difficult of Kierkegaard's books, this pseudonymous work develops his view on original sin and the relationship between sin and anxiety, which is analyzed as rooted in freedom and involving a fundamental attraction and repulsion for the same object.

Concluding Unscientific Postscripts, translated by David Swenson and Walter Lowrie (Princeton: Princeton University Press, 1941). Regarded as one of Kierkegaard's philosophical masterworks and soon to be retranslated, this book has a pseudonymous author who claims not to be a Christian but who has great interest in and respect for Christianity. It develops at great length Kierkegaard's special concept of "existence" and explores the role of suffering in the religious life, among other things.

Either/Or, vols. 1 and 2, translated by Howard V. Hong and Edna H. Hong (Princeton: Princeton University Press, 1987). This work dramatically presents the contrast between the aesthetic life and the ethical life by purporting to present the papers of representatives of each life-view in separate volumes. Volume 1 is rich in experiential descriptions of the despair in the aesthetic life, while volume 2 contains detailed analysis of the psychological problems of the aesthete.

Fear and Trembling and *Repetition*, translated by Howard V. Hong and Edna H. Hong (Princeton: Princeton University Press, 1983). Both books are pseudonymous "aesthetic" works. *Fear and Trembling* presents a vivid picture of the irreducibility of the religious life of faith to the ethical life through a look at Abraham's act in willing to sacrifice Isaac, an act that could only be justified by his trust that God had spoken to him. *Repetition* explores in a very oblique way how the religious life requires us to see our lives as something that must be re-created, rather than something already there that can simply be "recollected." This work is mainly a story about a broken love affair, in which the young lover tries to decide whether his love can be re-created or must be transformed into something else.

Søren Kierkegaard's Journals and Papers, seven volumes, translated by Howard V. Hong and Edna H. Hong (Bloomington: Indiana University Press, 1967–1978). These volumes are extremely valuable. The Hong translation groups entries related to a similar concept, with the concepts arranged alphabetically, so it is easy to find entries dealing with a particular topic, such as "anxiety" or "despair." Other volumes group entries that have biographical significance chronologically, and there is an excellent index volume.

The Point of View for My Work as An Author, translated by Walter Lowrie (New York: Harper & Row, 1962). Kierkegaard here gives his own account of his writing's purpose and overall structure. He is careful to admit that the books did not all originally have the meaning he sees at the end, and he attributes the happy (in his eyes) result to divine providence.

The Sickness unto Death, translated by Howard V. Hong and Edna H. Hong (Princeton: Princeton University Press, 1980). This is Kierkegaard's psychological masterwork, the book on which I have relied most heavily in the present volume. It is authored by the pseudonymous Anti-Climacus, who represents Christianity in its highest and strictest form.

Training in Christianity, translated by Walter Lowrie (Princeton: Princeton University Press, 1944). This second work by Anti-Climacus describes the Christian life as necessarily involving opposition to the world, which is inherent in being a follower of Jesus instead of simply an admirer. It includes an important discussion of the nature of offense, which is the only real alternative to faith once one has encountered the gospel. Its new title in Princeton's *Kierke-gaard's Writings* series will be *Practice in Christianity*.

Works of Love, translated by Howard V. Hong and Edna H. Hong (New York: Harper & Row, 1962). Kierkegaard's most significant work on love, which is the heart of the Christian life. The first part defines and contrasts Christian love as neighbor love with other types of human love; the second part delineates how neighbor love expresses itself concretely.

Books About Kierkegaard

Since the secondary literature is immense, I will mention only a few books that I regard as specially valuable.

C. Stephen Evans, *Kierkegaard's Fragments and Postscripts* (Atlantic Highlands, N.J.: Humanities Press, 1983). The first two chapters of this book provide a clear introduction to Kierkegaard's writings. The remainder of the book deals with Kierkegaard's view of Christian faith, including his controversial claims about the Incarnation as the absolute paradox and the relationship of faith to history.

Walter Lowrie, *A Short Life of Kierkegaard* (Princeton: Princeton University Press, 1942). Though some have criticized Lowrie for overly charitable interpretations of Kierkegaard, I still prefer his sympathetic reading to some of the cynical, debunking contemporary biographies. Lowrie was a deeply spiritual man who appreciated Kierkegaard's spiritual development.

John Douglas Mullen, *Kierkegaard's Philosophy: Self-Deceit and Cowardice in the Present Age* (New York: NAL, 1981). This is an extremely well-written introduction to Kierkegaard that stresses his relevance to contemporary problems. Mullen does unfortunately accept a view of how Christian faith is chosen that seems overly "existentialist" to me.

Kresten Nordentoft, *Kierkegaard's Psychology*, translated by Bruce Kirmmse (Pittsburgh: Duquesne University Press, 1972). This is a long and difficult work, but it contains a wealth of valuable reflection on Kierkegaard as a psychological thinker.

Index

Printed in the United States
21750LVS00001B/415-426

9 781573 830386